Centering Equity in Your Organization

A Guide to Building Bridges Not Barriers for All Employees

Jenora Ledbetter

GREEN HEART
LIVING
— PRESS —

ISBN Paperback: 978-1-954493-68-1

Published by Green Heart Living Press

Cover design by Elizabeth B. Hill

To my loving family,

Thank you for your unwavering support and encouragement throughout my journey as a writer. Your belief in me has inspired me to pursue my passion and create something that I hope will make you proud. I could not have done this without your love, patience, and understanding.

To my dear friends,

You have been my rock, my sounding board, and my source of laughter and joy. Your support and feedback have been invaluable to me, and I feel so lucky to have you in my life. Thank you for always being there for me through thick and thin.

To my readers,

This book is for you. I hope it brings you joy, inspiration, and the knowledge to build strong, inclusive teams within your organization. Your enthusiasm and support mean the world to me, and I am honored to share my stories with you.

With love and gratitude,

Jenora Molette Ledbetter

Contents

Introduction

O nce upon a time, in the fast-paced world of corporate America, I embarked on a journey filled with challenges, microaggressions, and a burning desire for change. As a Black woman navigating the intricacies of the corporate landscape, I encountered numerous instances of subtle but hurtful biases known as microaggressions.

I vividly remember the day when my accomplishments were undermined by a colleague's dismissive comment. It was a seemingly harmless remark, but it pierced through my confidence like a thousand tiny daggers. The microaggressions continued, chipping away at my spirit, leaving me questioning my abilities and worth in a world that often failed to see beyond the color of my skin.

However, these experiences didn't break me. They ignited a fire within me—a fire fueled by a burning passion for justice, equity, and inclusion. The great divide I witnessed in the corporate world became the catalyst for my transformation. I knew that I had to take action and become an agent of change.

Driven by a desire to dismantle the systemic barriers that hindered marginalized individuals, I made the life-altering decision to start my own consulting firm. I recognized the urgent need for organizations to go beyond surface-level initiatives and truly embrace the principles of equity, inclusion, and belonging.

My consulting firm became a platform to bridge the divide, a place where I could empower organizations to dismantle the invisible barriers that kept talented individuals from reaching their full potential. I delved deep into research, learning the intricacies of bias, privilege, and unconscious discrimination. Armed with knowledge and fueled by personal experiences, I set out to create lasting change.

Through workshops, training sessions, and one-on-one consultations, I helped organizations recognize the impact of their unconscious biases and foster inclusive cultures. I worked tirelessly to cultivate empathy, awareness, and understanding, urging leaders and employees alike to embrace the beauty and strength that lies in diversity.

My journey was not without challenges. I faced skepticism, resistance, and the occasional setback. But I never lost sight of my mission, for every success story I witnessed reaffirmed the importance of my work. Witnessing individuals' transformative journeys, the emergence of genuine connections, and the breaking down of barriers, I knew that my purpose was being fulfilled.

Centering Equity in Your Organization: A Guide to Building Bridges Not Barriers for All Employees, provides a comprehensive guide for organizations to create and implement effective equity, inclusion, belonging, and diversity (EIDB) strategies that promote a more inclusive and equitable workplace culture.

The content encompasses various areas, including grasping the rationale behind EIDB in business, recognizing and tackling bias and discrimination, cultivating inclusive leadership qualities, nurturing a sense of belonging and allyship, gauging the effects of EIDB endeavors, and managing situations when your organization and employees encounter EIDB fatigue.

The book also includes case studies, practical tools, and exercises to help organizations put the concepts into practice. Overall, the book provides a valuable resource for organizations looking to build more diverse, equitable, and inclusive workplaces.

First and foremost, equity, inclusion, belonging, and diversity are critical issues in today's workplace. Many companies recognize the importance of creating a equitable and inclusive workforce, not only for ethical reasons but also because it can lead to better business outcomes. Readers who are interested in promoting EIDB in their own workplaces may find this book to be a valuable resource.

Secondly, EIDB is a complex and multifaceted issue, and there is a lot of misinformation and misunderstanding surrounding it. This book helps readers gain a deeper understanding of the challenges and opportunities associated with promoting EIDB in the workplace. It also offers practical strategies and tools for addressing these challenges.

Finally, EIDB is an important social issue that goes beyond the workplace. Readers who are interested in promoting social justice and equality may find this book to be a valuable resource for understanding the broader societal implications of EIDB and how they can contribute to positive change.

Today, my consulting firm stands as a beacon of hope, offering guidance and support to organizations seeking to create inclusive environments where every individual, regardless of their background, feels seen, valued, and heard. The great divide that propelled me to start this journey has transformed into a bridge—one that connects people, ideas, and experiences, fostering a world where diversity is not merely tolerated but truly celebrated.

Chapter One

Leading with Equity

At The Self Care Network LLC, we understand that self-care is deeply intertwined with the environments in which individuals live and work. True well-being cannot be achieved in isolation from the societal structures that influence access to resources, opportunities, and a sense of belonging. We recognize that systemic inequities—whether in healthcare, education, the workplace, or broader societal structures—significantly impact individuals' ability to practice self-care and experience holistic well-being.

Equity, therefore, is not just a component of our work; it is the foundation upon which our entire approach is built. We lead with equity because we believe that without addressing the root causes of inequality, efforts to promote self-care will always be limited in their effectiveness. By prioritizing equity, we aim to dismantle the barriers that prevent individuals from accessing the care, support, and opportunities they need to thrive.

Our decision to lead with equity is driven by a commitment to addressing the systemic inequities that disproportionately affect marginalized communities. Whether it is in the workplace, in access to mental health resources, or in opportunities for personal and professional growth, we understand that not everyone starts from the same place.

For example, in the realm of mental health, we recognize that Black, Indigenous, and People of Color (BIPOC) communities often face significant barriers to accessing quality care, including cultural stigmas, lack of representation among mental health professionals, and financial constraints. Leading with equity means working to remove these barriers, advocating for culturally competent care, and ensuring that our consulting services are accessible and relevant to all communities.

In our workplace consulting, leading with equity involves helping organizations to critically examine their policies, practices, and cultures to identify and address inequities. We assist our clients in creating environments where all employees, regardless of their background, can access the resources they need to succeed and feel supported in their professional growth.

In recent years, the concept of Diversity, Equity, Inclusion, and Belonging (DEIB) has become a cornerstone of organizational culture and social justice efforts. These principles guide institutions in their pursuit of fairness, representation, and respect for all individuals, regardless of their background. However, there has been a growing conversation around the order in which these principles are presented and prioritized. Some advocates and thought leaders have begun to propose a shift from DEIB to EIBD—placing Equity at the forefront. This chapter explores the rationale behind this reordering, the significance of leading with equity, and how this shift can transform organizational cultures and society at large.

The Traditional DEIB Framework

The DEIB framework has served as a powerful tool for promoting a more inclusive and diverse environment. Each component plays a vital role:

- Diversity focuses on ensuring representation of various identities and perspectives.

- Equity seeks to provide fair treatment, opportunities, and outcomes for all individuals, recognizing that not everyone starts from the same place.

- Inclusion emphasizes the importance of creating environments where all individuals feel valued, respected, and able to contribute fully.

- Belonging is the ultimate goal—ensuring that everyone feels a deep sense of acceptance and community within the organization.

While this framework has been instrumental in driving progress, it is not without its limitations. Often, diversity initiatives are prioritized, with equity, inclusion, and belonging treated as secondary concerns. This can lead to situations where organizations are diverse on paper but fail to address systemic inequalities or create truly inclusive environments.

Why Lead with Equity?

Addressing the Root of Inequality

Equity, when placed at the forefront, shifts the focus from simply increasing representation to addressing the underlying structures that perpetuate inequality. Diversity without equity can lead to tokenism, where underrepresented groups are included without the necessary support or opportunities to thrive. By leading with equity, organizations commit to dismantling the barriers that have historically marginalized certain groups.

For example, in the workplace, equity might involve revising recruitment practices to ensure that they are not biased, implementing policies that support the advancement of underrepresented employees, and ensuring that all employees have access to the resources they need to succeed. Without equity, the other elements of DEIB—diversity, inclusion, and belonging—cannot be fully realized.

Ensuring Fairness in Outcomes

Equity is not just about providing equal opportunities; it is about ensuring that everyone has the resources and support they need to achieve fair outcomes. This means recognizing that different individuals may require different types of support to reach the same level of success.

In the context of education, for instance, equity might involve providing additional resources to schools in underfunded areas or offering mentorship programs for students from historically marginalized communities. In the corporate world, it could involve creating pathways for career advancement that specifically support employees from underrepresented groups.

When equity is prioritized, the focus shifts from merely creating diverse and inclusive environments to ensuring that all individuals have an equal chance to succeed. This is crucial in fostering a sense of belonging, as it demonstrates a commitment to fairness and justice.

Challenging Systemic Racism and Discrimination

Systemic racism and discrimination are deeply ingrained in many institutions and societies. These systems are maintained by inequitable practices that benefit some groups while putting others at a disadvantage. Leading with equity involves actively challenging and changing these systems.

For example, in the context of healthcare, leading with equity means recognizing and addressing the disparities in health outcomes between different racial and socioeconomic groups. This might involve implementing policies that ensure all patients receive the same level of care, regardless of their background, or developing programs to address the specific health needs of marginalized communities.

Incorporating equity as the foundation of organizational and societal practices requires a commitment to justice and a willingness to confront uncomfortable truths about power, privilege, and oppression. It demands a proactive approach to identifying and dismantling systems of inequality, rather than simply reacting to their symptoms.

The Importance of the EIBD Model

A New Hierarchy of Priorities

Reordering the traditional DEIB framework to prioritize equity creates a new hierarchy that reflects the need to address systemic issues before attempting to build diversity, inclusion, and belonging. By leading with equity, organizations can ensure that their efforts in the other areas are built on a solid foundation of fairness and justice.

This approach recognizes that diversity is not an end in itself, but rather a means to achieving equity and inclusion. It also acknowledges that inclusion and belonging are not possible without first addressing the inequities that exist within the system. In this sense, the EIBD model offers a more holistic and effective approach to creating truly inclusive environments.

Aligning Intentions with Outcomes

One of the key advantages of the EIBD model is that it aligns organizational intentions with outcomes. By prioritizing equity, organizations can ensure that their diversity and inclusion efforts lead to meaningful change. This is particularly important in addressing the "diversity fatigue" that can arise when efforts to increase representation do not result in tangible benefits for marginalized groups.

For example, a company might implement a diversity initiative that successfully increases the representation of women and people of color in leadership positions. However, without a focus on equity, these individuals may still face significant barriers to success, such as unequal pay, lack of mentorship opportunities, or a hostile work environment. By leading with equity, organizations can ensure that their diversity efforts are accompanied by the necessary support and resources to achieve fair outcomes.

Promoting a Culture of Accountability

The EIBD model also promotes a culture of accountability. When equity is placed at the forefront, organizations are more likely to adopt policies and practices that hold leaders and employees accountable for their actions. This might include implementing regular equity audits, setting measurable goals for equity and inclusion, and creating mechanisms for reporting and addressing discrimination and bias. In this way, the EIBD model helps to create a culture of continuous improvement and responsibility, where everyone within the organization is committed to advancing equity. This accountability ensures that the goals of equity, inclusion, diversity, and belonging are not just aspirational but are actively pursued and realized. It also fosters transparency, as organizations are encouraged to regularly assess and report on their progress, making them more responsive to the needs and concerns of all stakeholders.

Transforming Organizational Culture

When equity is prioritized, it fundamentally transforms organizational culture. Rather than simply ticking boxes or meeting quotas, organizations become places where all employees feel supported, valued, and empowered to succeed. This shift not only enhances employee satisfaction and retention but also drives innovation and creativity, as diverse perspectives are more effectively integrated into decision-making processes.

Moreover, an equity-first approach helps to cultivate trust within the organization. Employees are more likely to feel confident in the organization's commitment to their well-being when they see that it is actively working to address inequities. This trust is essential for fostering a sense of belonging and for creating an environment where all voices are heard and respected.

Resistance to Change

One of the most significant challenges in shifting from DEIB to EIBD is resistance to change. Organizations that have long operated under the traditional DEIB framework may be reluctant to reorder their priorities, especially if they believe that their current approach is already effective. Additionally, there may be concerns about the implications of leading with equity, particularly if it requires significant changes to existing practices and policies.

Overcoming this resistance requires strong leadership and a clear articulation of the benefits of leading with equity. It also involves engaging all stakeholders in the process, ensuring that everyone understands the rationale for the change and is committed to its success.

Balancing Equity with Other Priorities

Another challenge is balancing equity with the other components of the DEIB framework. While equity is essential, it is also important to ensure that diversity, inclusion, and belonging are not neglected. The EIBD model does not suggest that these elements are less important, but rather that they must be pursued within an equitable framework.

To achieve this balance, organizations must take a holistic approach that integrates equity into all aspects of their DEIB efforts. This might involve revising existing diversity and inclusion initiatives to ensure they are grounded in equity or developing new programs and policies that simultaneously address all four components of the EIBD model.

Measuring Success

Measuring the success of equity initiatives can be challenging, particularly because equity is often more difficult to quantify than diversity or inclusion. While diversity can be measured through representation metrics, and inclusion through employee engagement surveys, equity requires a more nuanced approach that takes into account the impact of policies and practices on different groups.

To effectively measure equity, organizations must develop comprehensive metrics that assess both process and outcomes. This might include tracking the distribution of resources and opportunities across different groups, evaluating the impact of equity-focused initiatives on marginalized communities, and regularly assessing employee experiences and perceptions of fairness.

The shift from DEIB to EIBD represents more than just a reordering of principles; it signifies a fundamental change in how organizations approach the pursuit of justice and fairness. By leading with equity, organizations can address the root causes of inequality, ensure fair outcomes for all, and create environments where diversity, inclusion, and belonging can truly thrive.

In an increasingly complex and diverse world, the importance of equity-first leadership cannot be overstated. It is not only a moral imperative but also a strategic one, as organizations that prioritize equity are better positioned to innovate, adapt, and succeed in a rapidly changing landscape.

Ultimately, leading with equity is about more than just achieving organizational goals; it is about contributing to a more just and equitable society. It is a commitment to ensuring that everyone, regardless of their background or circumstances, has the opportunity to succeed and thrive. And it is a recognition that true diversity, inclusion, and belonging are only possible when equity is at the forefront.

As we move forward, it is essential that we continue to challenge ourselves and our organizations to lead with equity, to hold ourselves accountable, and to strive for a world where fairness and justice are the norm, not the exception.

Case Study

Implementing an Equity-First Approach at The Self Care Network LLC

Background

The Self Care Network LLC was approached by a mid-sized healthcare organization struggling with employee retention and low morale among its frontline workers, particularly those from marginalized backgrounds. Despite having a diverse workforce, they faced challenges in creating an environment where all employees felt valued, supported, and able to thrive. The leadership recognized the need to shift from focusing solely on diversity initiatives to a more comprehensive strategy that addressed the systemic inequities impacting their employees' well-being and professional growth.

Challenges

- **High Turnover Rates Among Marginalized Employees**: The organization had a higher turnover rate among BIPOC employees and those from lower socioeconomic backgrounds compared to their white counterparts. Many employees cited a lack of career advancement opportunities, inequitable workloads, and a feeling of being undervalued as reasons for leaving.

- **Inequitable Access to Resources**: While the organization offered several resources for professional development and well-being, these were not equally accessible to all employees. For example, frontline workers, who were predominantly BIPOC, often could not take advantage of professional development opportunities due to their demanding schedules and lack of coverage.

- **Lack of Culturally Competent Care and Training**: The organization had received feedback from both employees and patients that their services were not always culturally competent. This lack of understanding and training among staff contributed to a less inclusive environment, both for employees and the patients they served.

The Self Care Network LLC's Equity-First Approach

After conducting a comprehensive assessment, The Self Care Network LLC proposed an equity-first strategy to address the identified challenges. This strategy focused on three key areas: 1) equitable access to resources, 2) culturally competent care and training, and 3) fostering an inclusive environment that promoted career advancement for all employees.

Step 1: Equitable Access to Resources

Objective: Ensure all employees, regardless of their role or background, have access to professional development and well-being resources.

- **Flexible Scheduling**: The Self Care Network LLC worked with the organization to implement more flexible scheduling options for frontline workers. This included staggered shifts and increased cross-training among staff to ensure that employees could attend professional development sessions without negatively impacting their workload.

- **Resource Equity Audits:** Regular audits were introduced to assess the distribution and accessibility of resources across different employee groups. These audits helped identify disparities in access and informed adjustments to ensure equitable distribution.

- **Targeted Professional Development Programs:** Tailored programs were created to address the specific needs and challenges faced by marginalized employees. These included mentorship programs, leadership training focused on equity, and workshops on navigating workplace challenges as a BIPOC employee.

Step 2: Culturally Competent Care and Training

Objective: Improve the organization's ability to provide culturally competent care, thus enhancing the work environment and patient experience.

- **Comprehensive Cultural Competency Training**: The Self Care Network LLC developed and implemented a mandatory training program on cultural competency for all staff. This program covered topics such as implicit bias, culturally sensitive communication, and understanding the specific health needs of diverse patient populations.

- **Diverse Patient Advocacy Groups**: The organization established patient advocacy groups made up of members from diverse communities. These groups provided feedback on care practices and helped the organization better understand and address the needs of different patient demographics.

- **Ongoing Support and Learning**: To reinforce the training, The Self Care Network LLC set up a series of follow-up workshops and discussions, allowing staff to share experiences, challenges, and strategies for continued improvement in culturally competent care.

Step 3: Promoting Career Advancement and Inclusion

Objective: Foster a more inclusive environment by creating equitable opportunities for career advancement and ensuring all employees feel valued.

- **Transparent Promotion Paths**: The Self Care Network LLC helped the organization establish clear, transparent criteria for promotions. These criteria were communicated to all employees, and managers were trained on how to support the career development of their teams equitably.

- **Mentorship and Sponsorship Programs**: A mentorship program was introduced, pairing marginalized employees with senior leaders in the organization. Additionally, a sponsorship program was created to actively advocate for high-potential employees from underrepresented groups in leadership discussions.

- **Inclusive Leadership Training**: Managers and leaders underwent training on inclusive leadership practices, focusing on how to create supportive, equitable teams where all voices are heard and valued.

Results

Within 18 months of implementing the equity-first strategy, the organization experienced significant positive changes:

- **Reduced Turnover**: The turnover rate among BIPOC employees and frontline workers decreased by 30%. Exit interviews revealed that employees felt more supported, valued, and hopeful about their career prospects within the organization.

- **Improved Employee Satisfaction**: Employee satisfaction scores improved by 25%, particularly in areas related to access to professional development and perceptions of fairness and inclusion.

- **Enhanced Cultural Competency**: Patient feedback indicated a marked improvement in the cultural sensitivity and competence of care provided by the organization. This led to higher patient satisfaction rates, especially among patients from diverse backgrounds.

- **Increased Representation in Leadership**: The proportion of BIPOC employees in leadership positions grew by 15%, reflecting the success of the mentorship, sponsorship, and professional development programs.

This case demonstrates the transformative power of leading with equity. By prioritizing equitable access to resources, fostering a culturally competent environment, and promoting career advancement for all employees, The Self Care Network LLC helped the organization not only improve retention and employee satisfaction but also create a more inclusive and supportive workplace. This equity-first approach not only benefited the employees but also enhanced the quality of care provided to the patients they served, illustrating the broader impact of prioritizing equity in organizational practices.

Integrative Exercise

Designing an Equity-First Strategy for Organizational Transformation

This exercise is designed to help participants understand and apply an equity-first approach to organizational transformation. Participants will work through real-world scenarios to develop strategies that address systemic inequities in a fictional organization. The goal is to integrate concepts of equity, diversity, inclusion, and belonging (EIBD) into a comprehensive plan that fosters a fair and supportive environment for all employees.

Target Audience: This exercise is suitable for leadership teams, DEIB practitioners, HR professionals, and organizational consultants.

Duration: 2-3 hours

Step 1: Understanding the Current Landscape (45 minutes)

Scenario Overview: You are part of a consulting team hired by a healthcare organization facing challenges similar to those described in the case study. The organization has a diverse workforce but struggles with high turnover among marginalized employees, inequitable access to resources, and low morale.

Current State Analysis

- Break into small groups (3-4 participants per group).

- Each group should spend 20 minutes analyzing the current state of the organization based on the following data points:

  - **Turnover Rates**: 35% higher among BIPOC employees and frontline workers.

- ○ **Employee Satisfaction**: Low scores in fairness, career advancement opportunities, and cultural competency of leadership.

- ○ **Patient Feedback**: Concerns about the lack of culturally competent care, especially from marginalized communities.

- ○ **Resource Access**: Discrepancies in access to professional development programs between frontline and administrative staff.

Discussion Questions

- What are the key challenges the organization is facing regarding equity?

- How do these challenges impact the organization's overall effectiveness, employee well-being, and patient care?

- Identify specific systemic inequities that need to be addressed.

Group Sharing

- Each group will present their analysis to the larger group, summarizing the key challenges and systemic inequities they identified. (10 minutes)

Step 2: Designing an Equity-First Strategy (60 minutes)

Developing Solutions: Groups will now focus on designing a comprehensive equity-first strategy for the organization. This should include specific initiatives, programs, or policies to address the identified challenges. Spend 40 minutes on this task.

Key Areas to Address

- **Equitable Access to Resources**: What changes can be made to ensure all employees have fair access to professional development, career advancement, and well-being resources?

- **Culturally Competent Care**: How can the organization improve the cultural competency of its staff and care practices?

- **Promoting Inclusion and Belonging**: What strategies can the organization implement to create an inclusive environment where all employees feel valued and supported?

- **Accountability and Measurement**: How will the organization measure the success of these initiatives and hold leadership accountable for maintaining equity?

Action Plan Components

- **Specific Initiatives**: Detail at least three initiatives the organization should implement.

- **Timeline**: Propose a timeline for rolling out these initiatives.

- **Stakeholder Engagement**: Identify key stakeholders and how they will be involved.

- **Metrics for Success**: Define clear metrics to evaluate the effectiveness of the equity-first strategy.

Group Presentations

- Each group will present their equity-first strategy to the larger group. Presentations should be 5-7 minutes each, followed by 3 minutes for questions and feedback from the audience.

Step 3: Reflection and Integration (30 minutes)

Individual Reflection

Take 10 minutes for individual reflection. Consider the following questions:

- How did leading with equity influence your approach to solving the organization's challenges?

- What insights did you gain about the importance of equity in creating sustainable organizational change?

- How can you apply these insights to your current role or organization?

Group Discussion

- Reconvene as a large group for a 20-minute discussion. Each participant should share one key takeaway from the exercise and how they plan to apply it in their professional practice.

Closing Thoughts

- The facilitator will summarize the key points discussed during the exercise, emphasizing the importance of an equity-first approach in achieving lasting organizational change. Participants will be encouraged to continue exploring and advocating for equity in their own organizations.

   This integrative exercise allows participants to move beyond theoretical understanding and apply equity-first principles in a practical, hands-on way. By designing a strategy for a fictional organization facing real-world challenges, participants develop the skills and confidence needed to lead with equity in their own workplaces, ultimately contributing to more just and inclusive environments.

Chapter Two

Organizational Growth through EIBD

In this chapter, we embark on a journey to explore the fundamental concepts of equity, inclusion, belonging, and diversity (EIBD) and their significance in building an inclusive organization. We delve into the essential principles of equity, unpacking its distinction from equality and emphasizing the value it adds to nurturing a diverse and thriving workplace. Understanding equity, inclusion, belonging, and diversity lays the groundwork for fostering an equitable and inclusive culture that promotes fairness, empowers all employees, and bridges the gaps that hinder progress toward a truly inclusive and equitable organization.

Throughout this book, I will be using the terms EIBD (Equity, Inclusion, Belonging, and Diversity) and DEIB (Diversity, Equity, Inclusion, and Belonging) interchangeably. While both acronyms encompass the same fundamental concepts, the slight variation in the order of terms reflects different emphases that organizations or individuals might prioritize within the broader framework of social justice and organizational change.

EIBD places 'Equity' and 'Inclusion' at the forefront, suggesting a focus on creating fair and inclusive environments before addressing diversity. This approach highlights the importance of ensuring that everyone has access to the same opportunities and resources and that they feel genuinely included and valued, which ultimately fosters a sense of belonging. By prioritizing these elements, EIBD emphasizes that diversity, while critical, is most effective and meaningful when equity and inclusion are well-established.

On the other hand, DEIB starts with 'Diversity,' placing an initial emphasis on the representation of different identities and perspectives. This approach often begins with recognizing and celebrating the variety of experiences and backgrounds that individuals bring to the table, followed by efforts to create equitable and inclusive environments where those diverse voices can thrive. In this framework, belonging is seen as the ultimate goal, achieved through the successful integration of diversity, equity, and inclusion efforts.

In practice, both EIBD and DEIB aim to achieve the same outcome: a work or community environment where all individuals feel valued, respected, and supported, regardless of their identity or background. The interchangeable use of these terms in this book acknowledges that while the order of priorities may vary, the end goal remains consistent. Whether starting from a place of equity or diversity, the ultimate aim is to create a holistic culture of belonging where every person can contribute and succeed

What is diversity, equity, inclusion, and belonging? We hear those words tossed around, but do we really understand what they mean? They can mean something different to everyone. Each person views them through their own perspective and worldview.

In this chapter, you will be introduced to the definitions of diversity, equity, inclusion, and belonging and why they are important in every working environment.

We are all functions of this system that we live in. It teaches us how we think about ourselves, how we think about others, and how we interact with others. It also teaches us how we understand what is expected of us. These are the thought processes that we've developed based on our environment, our parents, our religion, our friends, and other factors. When this happens, this is when we develop our thought processes based on these different social identities and how we define ourselves. We suddenly have unequal roles in this environment that either allow us to have access to resources or deny us access to resources.

In referencing EIBD, we're talking about creating and maintaining a successful workplace where people can come to work and can be authentically themselves. This allows employees to thrive in their work environment.

Before you begin doing this very important work of EIBD, you must understand what EIBD is, how you create those definitions within your organization, and how you will embed them into your workplace.

In order to lead with equity, it is crucial to first understand how the acronyms of DEIB came to be and what they signify within the broader social and historical context. The concepts of diversity, equity, inclusion, and belonging did not emerge in isolation; they are the result of decades of advocacy, scholarship, and lived experiences, particularly within marginalized communities. Each term within these acronyms represents a specific aspect of the struggle for social justice and equal opportunity. Understanding the historical and social roots of these terms allows leaders to grasp the complexities of equity and to apply these principles in ways that are both informed and impactful.

Let's clarify DEIB definitions.

What is Diversity?

Diversity is defined as having a workplace with differences in race, ethnicity, gender, gender identity, sexual orientation, age, socio-economic class, and differences in physical ability and diversity of thought.

Organizations that desire diversity in their workplace welcome different perspectives, different life experiences, and different lived experiences. These all provide the staff with new perspectives on how workplaces will write their policies and procedures and execute their processes. Having diverse voices leads to better outcomes in those organizations because they're creating a space where everyone is able to see something through a different lens and still come together as a well-blended unit.

There are four types of diversity: internal, external, worldview, and organizational.

Internal diversity refers to the different characteristics someone is born with. This can include their sex, ethnicity, nationality, gender, race, physical or mental ability, and sexual orientation. In the workplace, it is not uncommon for an employee to be discriminated against based on their race, gender, or sexual orientation.

External diversity refers to experiences or circumstances that define a person's identity outside of the characteristics they were born with. This can include socioeconomic status, marital status, religion, appearance, or educational background. These are characteristics that can be consciously changed.

Worldview diversity refers to a broad range of beliefs, political affiliations, travel experiences, and cultures. Anything in our environment that influences the way we process and view the world is part of worldview diversity.

Organizational diversity refers to the way the workforce views its employees. These differences include work experience, management level, seniority, and job functions. It is not uncommon for organizations to have departments or positions within the organization that are homogeneous. We tend to see this a lot in leadership positions, where organizations do not tend to have many people of color in executive positions.

Organizations that put diversity at the forefront of their organizational initiatives are more likely to have higher revenue growth, higher employee retention, and greater readiness to innovate. Clients and customers are more likely to do business with an organization where they see themselves represented.

Let's take a moment to reflect on how effectively your organization promotes diversity by answering the following questions.

- How diverse is your executive team?

- What percentage of your staff would agree that the workplace is diverse?

- Does your company culture celebrate diverse ideas and people?

- How well does your Human Resource department work toward hiring candidates from diverse backgrounds?

- How do you think the organization can improve its diversity efforts in the future?

Diversity supports the organization's growth because it allows differences to become strengths. Different perspectives and mindsets can offer new ideas, innovations, wisdom, vitality, spirited discussions, and much more.

What is Equity?

Equity is generally defined as ensuring that processes and programs are impartial and fair, providing equal possible outcomes for every individual. Within the workplace, this is providing people with what they need at work while recognizing that each person is going to have different circumstances and different needs. These differences in people are going to need a variety of resources and opportunities allocated to them in order to thrive.

Within the traditional systems of management, senior leadership manages their teams with the belief that every employee needs the same support and the same resources. If employees are not thriving or doing their job, senior leadership will place their employees on a performance improvement plan without acknowledging that performance improvement plans focus on symptoms, not root problems.

When we talk about bringing equity into an organization, senior leadership should have an open dialogue with the struggling employees and search for the areas where they need support. Do they have a learning disability? Do they process information differently than the others on their team? Do they struggle with reading or comprehension? What is their learning style—auditory, visual, or kinesthetic? Do they need someone to speak the instructions to understand? (Auditory.) Do they need visuals like written words, charts, and graphs to understand best what is expected? (Visual.) Would hands-on learning with active participation work best for them? (Kinesthetic.)

Installing these support systems into the team will be more productive than automatically assuming that you have someone on your team that doesn't know how to do the job, or they are lazy.

In order to bring equity into an organization, leaders need to understand the different levels of racism and how they operate within society.

Structural Racism

Structural racism is a system where institutional practices and public policies reinforce ways to perpetuate racial group inequality. It includes societal factors such as history, culture, and interactions of systematically privileged white people and disadvantaged people of color. Structural racism shows up in the workplace when a person of color's professional development and career advancements are stifled. It can show up in an organization's inequitable pay scales. Historically BIPOC (Black, Indigenous, and People of Color) employees are paid less than white employees with the same degree and experience. Structural racism may also show up in an organization's recruitment practices. A study has found that Black-sounding names were less likely to get a call back from recruiters vs. white-sounding names.

Institutional racism is the system in place within organizations that continues to produce racially inequitable outcomes for people of color and advantages for white people. It includes unfair policies and practices, inequitable opportunities, and discriminatory treatment based on race. Institutional racism is deeply embedded in corporate culture. The BIPOC community may receive less favorable treatment at work. Within many organizations, day-to-day operations and hiring and firing practices can significantly disadvantage employees of color.

Although senior leadership may be excited to embrace equity within their organizations, there are often challenges they face when getting started. Many white leaders may fear saying or doing something wrong. They may have a fear that they are perceived as not being the right type of person to discuss issues around race and equity within an organization. Leaders of color may be fearful of speaking up or rocking the boat, especially when they work for predominantly white-dominant organizations. Employees who are not in leadership positions can also initiate discussions about racial equity. It is important for organizations to find at least one other person in the organization that supports the work.

Interpersonal racism is racism between individuals. It occurs when individuals interact, and their private beliefs affect their interactions. This shows up a lot in the workplace when a person is allowing their implicit bias to drive their decisions, actions, and behaviors. We will take a deeper look at implicit bias in the next few chapters.

Personal racism can be defined as the private beliefs, ideas, or prejudices that an individual has about the superiority of whites and the inferiority of people of color. For people of color, it shows up as internalized oppression. For whites, it shows up as internalized racial superiority. This can show up in the workplace in different ways. A BIPOC employee might become an overachiever at work because they are extremely grateful to be given a chance and want to prove to everyone that they deserve to be there. They may also suppress aspects of their race at work to avoid looking or sounding too ethnic. For white employees, this can show up as voicing their opinions at a meeting and interrupting colleagues of color. It may also show up as refusing to participate in DEIB initiatives at work because a person does not want to be made to feel ignorant, sad, guilty, or ashamed.

Building equity within an organization requires an understanding of the history and background of structural racism. In order to build equity, organizations will need to accept the historical and ongoing disparities of their internal policies and procedures and take steps to mitigate those inequities through positive action.

Equity supports the organization when they no longer filter resumes by the way an applicant's name appears. Instead of bypassing someone who might be the best person for the job simply because they have a difficult-to-pronounce or ethnic-sounding name. Equity opens their mindset to consider all candidates based solely on the applicant's merits and qualifications. When judgments stop by removing the bias according to someone's name, appearance, or how they speak, organizations will flourish with an influx of the right people for the right job.

Let's take a moment to reflect on how effectively your organization promotes equity by answering the following questions.

- Do your employees feel equally paid, honored, validated, and heard?

- Do your employees believe they are being treated fairly and with respect in the workplace?

- How do you prioritize social events that all employees feel they can take part in?

- What steps or initiatives could your organization take to pursue or achieve equity?

- Are there current measures of success you could point to as evidence of these efforts?

The Difference Between Equity and Equality in Organizational Contexts

While equity and equality are often used interchangeably in everyday conversations, they represent two distinct approaches to fairness and justice. Equality focuses on providing the same resources or opportunities to everyone, regardless of their individual needs or starting points. It operates on the premise that everyone benefits from the same level of support. However, this approach can overlook the systemic barriers and disadvantages that some individuals or groups face. On the other hand, equity recognizes that people start from different places and require varying levels of support to achieve similar outcomes. It involves distributing resources and opportunities based on individual needs, acknowledging that a one-size-fits-all approach may not lead to true fairness.

Many organizations struggle with this distinction, often confusing equality with equity in their policies and practices. This confusion can lead to well-intentioned but ineffective strategies that fail to address the unique challenges faced by marginalized communities. For instance, an organization might implement an equality-based approach by offering the same professional development opportunities to all employees. While this may seem fair on the surface, it ignores the fact that employees from underrepresented groups may require additional support or different types of resources to overcome systemic barriers and fully benefit from these opportunities. Without a clear understanding of equity, organizations risk perpetuating existing disparities rather than correcting them, which can undermine their efforts to create truly inclusive and just environments.

What is Inclusion?

Inclusion is defined as the practice of ensuring that people feel a sense of belonging in the workplace. Every employee should feel comfortable and supported by the organization to show up as themselves.

Organizations may say their employees are encouraged to be authentically themselves, but they may not always *intend* for employees to follow through.

Organizations that practice inclusion encourage employees to be themselves authentically and help them feel comfortable in doing so. They are valued at work by their peers and employers. The organization makes sure they feel welcomed by feeling acknowledged.

If there is only one employee of color at an organization or in a particular department, they may begin to question the authenticity of themselves and that of the organization.

People really want to feel that they belong. Marginalized groups want to know that they're not going to be the token person to represent a demographic. Organizations should focus on how they want their employees of color to have an impact within the company and less on the color of their skin.

Let's take a look at some of the building blocks that set the foundation of inclusivity within an organization.

Do your employees feel valued? Employees who don't feel valued at work may begin to question if their efforts and contributions are being noticed.

I remember interviewing at a non-profit organization that informed me in the interview that they were looking for a diversity hire to bring innovative ideas and thinking into the organization. However, once I was hired, it was a different environment than what they portrayed to me in the interview. I was the only person of color on the leadership team, and my ideas were continuously shot down. As a woman of color, I felt devalued and tokenized.

It is also important for organizations to ensure that all employees have access to the same resources. Employees should have access to training, company policies and procedures, and support from senior leadership.

Lastly, organizations should make sure that every process and procedure follows inclusive practices. Strategic alignment is important for senior leadership to provide transparency to their employees.

Inclusion supports the organization when people feel the freedom to be their authentic selves. Freedom to be authentic opens minds to creative and innovative ideas. If employees feel that all are included, this can become the melting pot for variety and creative innovation. Studies have shown that a happy, inclusive workplace gives way to higher productivity, less turnover, and better health for employees.

Let's take a moment to reflect on how effectively your organization promotes inclusion by answering the following questions.

- Do your employees believe your organization is inclusive and feel they can express their true, authentic selves? If they do, are they welcomed in their truest sense of personality and expression of their feelings?

- Do your organization's training methods promote inclusivity?

- Do your employees feel confident enough to discuss their opinions at work?

- How does your organization define inclusion?

- Are all employees included in business decisions that impact their work?

What is Belonging?

In the ever-evolving landscape of DEIB, the concept of "belonging" takes center stage as an essential component of creating thriving and inclusive environments. Let's explore the significance of fostering a sense of belonging within DEIB initiatives, exploring its multifaceted dimensions and practical applications in organizations.

Understanding Belonging

Belonging goes beyond mere inclusion; it encapsulates the feeling of being welcomed, valued, and able to be one's authentic self. It's about creating an environment where individuals not only have a seat at the table but also feel that their voices matter and that they are an integral part of the community. To make progress, organizations need to measure the sense of belonging within their workforce. Belonging isn't achieved overnight, and there can be challenges along the way. In this book, we discuss common hurdles, such as resistance to change and DEIB fatigue, and provide strategies for overcoming these obstacles.

Let's take a moment to reflect on how effectively your organization promotes belonging by answering the following questions.

- What support systems are in place to help employees overcome any barriers or biases they may encounter in the workplace?

- Are there visible and accessible mentorship or sponsorship programs that help employees from underrepresented groups advance in their careers?

- Do leaders and managers actively promote and engage in conversations about diversity, equity, inclusion, and belonging?

- What initiatives or programs are in place to build bridges and foster connections among employees from different backgrounds and experiences?

- How does the organization address DEIB fatigue and ensure that employees remain engaged and committed to these efforts over time?

When organizations strive to center equity within their framework, they should adopt the EIBD (Equity, Inclusion, Belonging, and Diversity) model as a foundational building block, where each component strengthens and supports the other. By intentionally building on EIBD, organizations create a cohesive, supportive culture that not only prioritizes fairness but also thrives on the strengths that true equity, inclusion, belonging, and diversity bring to the table.

What are the Federally Protected Classes?

Federally protected classes are groups of individuals who are legally safeguarded against discrimination in various aspects of life under U.S. federal law. These protections are intended to ensure equal treatment and opportunities. The main federally protected classes include:

- **Race**—pertains to the set of physical characteristics, i.e., African American, Black, Asian, White, Native American, Native Hawaiian, Pacific Islander, Aboriginal, etc.

- **Ethnicity**—pertains to culture in language, ancestral practices, and beliefs, i.e., Russian, Dutch, Chinese, Japanese, Latino, Native American, Jamaican, etc.

- **Age**—pertains to the number of years someone has lived.

- **Sex**—pertaining to biological differences of male, female, and intersex.

- **Sexual Orientation**—pertains to the gender to which a person is attracted sexually.

- **National Origin or Ancestry**—pertains to the defining country for citizenship at birth.

- **Gender Identity**—pertains to the person's perception of having a particular gender.

- **Ability**—pertaining to physical, psychological, and mental ability versus disability.

- **Veteran Status**—pertains to someone who has served on active duty in the United States military armed forces of any branch.

- **Citizenship**—pertains to someone's current status of citizenship.

- **Religion**—pertains to a person's particular system of faith or worship.

Measuring Your Workplace Culture

Measuring workplace culture is essential for understanding the values, beliefs, behaviors, and overall atmosphere within an organization. Effective measurement can provide insights into areas of strength and areas that require improvement.

How do your employees perceive the work culture within your organization? Is it a place of innovation and acceptance? Or does it limit and devalue employees?

Since most states are at-will employment or right-to-work states, what would deem an employee not a good fit? What would cause your leadership to release an employee? What message are you expressing to your employees through your company culture? Are you standing for Diversity, Equity, Inclusion, and Belonging?

If you have a hard time answering these questions, then this could be a sign of a bigger issue. A weak culture signifies that there are cracks in the organization that need to be examined. On occasion, you may hear employees describe their work culture as *the way we do things around here.* Policies and procedures are enforced to ensure that departments are running smoothly. In order to develop the culture, you need to develop systems. Without systems, an organization will be unable to achieve organizational goals.

A Diversity, Equity, Inclusion, and Belonging (DEIB) assessment is a comprehensive evaluation tool used by organizations to measure and analyze the effectiveness of their DEIB policies and practices. These assessments are crucial to determine how well an organization fosters an environment where diverse individuals feel respected, included, and valued.

Here's what each component typically measures:

- **Diversity:** This part of the assessment evaluates the demographic makeup of an organization, including race, gender, ethnicity, age, sexual orientation, disability status, and more. It assesses whether the organization reflects the broader society and the industries in which it operates and whether there are equitable opportunities for all.

- **Equity:** This measures the fairness and impartiality of the organization's policies and practices. It looks at how resources and opportunities are distributed to ensure that all individuals, particularly those from historically marginalized groups, have the support they need to succeed. This includes reviewing wage gaps, promotion rates, and access to professional development.

- **Inclusion:** This assesses the extent to which diverse employees feel valued and integrated within the organization. It typically involves surveys and interviews to gauge employees' sense of belonging and their perceptions of the organizational culture, including whether diverse viewpoints are respected and incorporated into decision-making processes.

- **Belonging:** Often seen as a part of inclusion, belonging specifically measures how individuals feel personally accepted, respected, and supported in their work environment. It looks at emotional experiences and personal engagement within the workplace, determining if employees truly feel they are an integral part of the organization.

Organizations use DEIB assessments to identify areas of strength and opportunities for improvement. By understanding the current state of DEIB within their structure, organizations can develop targeted strategies to enhance diversity, ensure equitable treatment, support inclusion, and foster a sense of belonging for all employees. These assessments are crucial for promoting an environment where all members feel they can thrive and contribute to their fullest potential.

Case Study

Diversity and Inclusion Training at Starbucks

In 2018, Starbucks faced a major controversy when employees at a Philadelphia store called the police on two African-American men who were waiting for a friend without making a purchase. The incident sparked protests and a national conversation about racial profiling and discrimination in public spaces.

In response to the incident, Starbucks CEO Kevin Johnson announced that the company would close more than 8,000 company-owned stores in the United States for an afternoon of racial bias training. The training, which took place in May 2018, was designed to help employees understand their unconscious biases and how to create a more inclusive environment for customers.

The training was developed in partnership with experts in the fields of diversity, equity, and inclusion and was delivered to more than 175,000 employees across the United States. The curriculum included a short documentary film, small-group discussions, and interactive exercises designed to help employees recognize their unconscious biases and understand the impact of their actions on others.

The training was not without its critics, with some arguing that a single afternoon of training was not enough to address the systemic issues of racism and discrimination in society. However, Starbucks viewed the training as a first step in a larger effort to create a more inclusive workplace and customer experience.

Since the training, Starbucks has continued to invest in diversity and inclusion initiatives, including the creation of an online curriculum for employees, the establishment of a diversity and inclusion advisory council, and increased representation of underrepresented groups in leadership positions.

The Starbucks case study illustrates the importance of addressing issues of diversity, equity, and inclusion in the workplace and the potential impact of training programs in creating a more inclusive culture. However, it also highlights the need for ongoing efforts to address systemic issues of discrimination and bias in society.

Integrative Exercise

Diversity, Equity, Inclusion, and Belonging

This exercise focuses on building the gap between generational diversity in the workforce. Employees who grew up in different eras have vastly different opinions on race, employee equity, and gender, which can sometimes lead to implicit bias and create non-welcoming environments.

Step 1: Diversity

In this exercise, have each group answer the following questions:

- What stereotypes do you hear the most about someone in your age group?

- How do these stereotypes impact the way you feel?

- What stereotypes do you agree with and why?

- What stereotypes do you not agree with and why?

- What makes you proud of being a member of your age group?

- What is one thing you are eager to learn about from people in other age groups?

Step 2: Equity

You are a supervisor at an organization. One of your team members, who is a Black female employee, has recently found out that she is being vastly underpaid compared to other employees who are in the same position as her in the organization. Your team members confide in you that she believes she is being discriminated against because of her race and gender.

In this exercise, have each group answer the following questions:

- How would you address this issue?

- What things could you say that would help the situation?

- What things could you say that would make the situation worse?

- How would you measure compensation to determine if there is a bias?

Step 3: Inclusion

Employees lived experiences outside of work inform the way they show up to work. We all want to feel included and accepted. By recognizing the lived experiences of employees organizations can create a safe space for their workforce to feel comfortable.

In a group setting, employees should complete the following statements and discussion topics:

- If you really knew me, you would know that I ...

- I feel the distinct challenges that I face due to my background (race, nationality, age, gender, sexual orientation, religion, disability status) are ...

- Discuss a time in your life when you felt valued and connected to others at work.

- Discuss a time in your life when you felt disconnected from others at work.

Step 4: Belonging

This scenario is designed to encourage individuals to take action to create a sense of belonging within their team.

You are a team member in a diverse workplace, and you've noticed that some of your colleagues from different cultural backgrounds often eat alone or bring their own food to work. You want to foster a sense of belonging and inclusion within your team. One day, during a team meeting, you decide to take action. At the end of the team meeting, when everyone is about to leave for lunch, you make an announcement:

"Hey everyone, I've noticed that some of us often eat alone or bring our own food to work. I think it would be great if we could have a team lunch together this Friday. We can each bring a dish that represents our cultural background and share a meal. It's a great way for us to learn more about each other's cultures and foster a stronger sense of belonging within our team."

You express your enthusiasm for the idea and encourage your colleagues to participate. You also suggest that if anyone prefers not to cook, they can bring a store-bought dish that represents their culture.

You take the initiative to coordinate the logistics, such as setting a date and time, creating a sign-up sheet for dishes, and finding a communal space to gather.

In the days leading up to the team lunch, you send reminder emails or messages to your colleagues and provide any necessary information or guidance for the event.

On the agreed-upon day, you and your colleagues come together for the team lunch. Everyone brings a dish, and you take this opportunity to share stories about the significance of the food in your respective cultures.

In a group setting, employees should complete the following statements and discussion topics:

- How important is it for your team to create a sense of belonging and inclusivity among its members?

- How would you react if a colleague like the one in the scenario suggested organizing a team lunch to foster belonging and cultural awareness?

- What strategies can your team employ to encourage participation in inclusive activities like a team lunch?

- How can team members support and collaborate with each other to make such initiatives successful?

Chapter Three

Bridging Civil Rights Equity and DEIB Assessments

I n this chapter, we explore the essential distinctions between DEIB assessments and Civil Rights Equity assessments. While both frameworks aim to promote fairness and inclusivity, they differ in their approaches and scopes. By understanding the unique focuses of these assessments, organizations can build a more comprehensive understanding of equity and identify synergies that lead to a more equitable workplace and society.

In this chapter, we will help you distinguish the differences and nuances of each to assist you in deciding what type of assessment is the most beneficial for your organization. Many organizations will choose to utilize both assessments; they each give support in slightly different ways. Each one measures different aspects, and this information will help you determine what you want to be measured in your organization.

Civil Rights Equity Audit

The fight for civil rights has been ongoing for centuries, and while significant progress has been made, the battle is far from over. To ensure equality and justice for all, it is essential to regularly assess and improve the policies and practices that govern our society. One effective tool for achieving this is the civil rights equity audit. This chapter will provide an overview of the civil rights equity audit and its importance in promoting equity and justice.

A civil rights equity audit is a comprehensive assessment of policies, practices, and procedures to determine their impact on marginalized communities. The audit examines the extent to which policies promote or impede equal opportunities for all individuals, regardless of their race, ethnicity, gender, sexual orientation, religion, disability, or other protected characteristics. The audit also evaluates the effectiveness of existing policies and identifies areas for improvement to ensure that they align with civil rights principles. Civil Rights Equity Audits were created by the US Equal Employment Opportunity Commission (EEOC). The EEOC is a federal anti-discrimination organization that promotes equal opportunity in the workplace.

The Civil Rights Equity Audit is a comprehensive review of the employer's practices related to issues such as recruitment, hiring, promotions, discipline, benefits, and wages in order to weed out discriminatory practices.

A Civil Rights Equity Audit helps an organization identify areas where changes need to be made so that employees have equal access to opportunities and makes sure that policies are promoting equality in all areas across the board by not discriminating against any particular group of people based on their identity or background.

This audit can also protect organizations from discrimination lawsuits by showing employees that the organization is making efforts to implement EIBD initiatives and follow equitable recruitment practices.

What is the purpose of Civil Rights Equity Audits?

A Civil Rights Equity Audit is an important tool for identifying and addressing systemic discrimination and inequities. It provides a framework for evaluating policies and practices through a lens of equity, which helps to ensure that they are fair, just, and inclusive. By conducting an audit, organizations can identify and address unconscious biases, disparities, and barriers to equity. This allows organizations to create policies and practices that promote equal opportunities for all individuals, which is critical for achieving a just and equitable society.

The goal of a Civil Rights Equity Audit is to examine institutional practices that produce discriminatory trends in data that affect employees. Organizations conduct audits to analyze data in several key areas: Recruitment, policies and procedures, promotions, benefits, and employee discipline and terminations.

Recruitment equity puts strategies into place to ensure that an organization's recruitment efforts are fostering a sense of inclusivity. An audit will examine an organization's applicant pool for the positions being offered so that it reflects the demographics of the community that the organization is serving. It is important for organizations to evaluate how positions being recruited can advance equity goals within the organization and how those expectations and responsibilities can be included in the recruitment process.

Equity policies focus on the need to eliminate disparities between underserved and underrepresented populations. It shifts the accountability to the organization rather than to the employee and allows the organization to see when policies and practices that appear to be beneficial are actually creating an inequitable environment. The audit examines company policies and procedures to assess the policy purpose and inclusiveness.

Equity in promotions is important to help an organization not only maintain diversity within its workforce but also to ensure that underrepresented groups are not being left behind. The audit examines the rate at which employees are being promoted within the organization with regard to diversity. If there is a lack of minorities in senior-level positions, this could indicate that this may be a problem that the organization needs to address.

Equitable benefits address the notion that not all employees need the same thing. It is important for an organization to understand if there are groups of employees that are being excluded from benefit programs. The audit will examine the benefits that are being offered to employees. Is there a pay disparity between women and men? Is there a pay disparity between minorities and non-minorities? As employees' expectations and workforce demographics change, applying an equity lens to workforce data can help an organization develop its benefits strategy.

Employment discrimination occurs when disparate treatment is present in situations where an employer treats some employees less favorably than others based on protected characteristics such as race or gender. Disparate discrimination treatment is usually the number one reason why an organization is faced with a discrimination lawsuit. The audit will examine employee discipline and terminations, looking for ways that the organization may possibly treat women and minorities differently when it comes to discipline or termination.

How is a Civil Rights Equity Audit Conducted?

A Civil Rights Equity Audit is typically conducted by a team of experts who specialize in civil rights law, policy analysis, and social justice advocacy. The audit involves a comprehensive review of policies, practices, and procedures, including hiring practices, promotion policies, programmatic activities, and service delivery mechanisms. The audit team analyzes data to identify disparities and examines the effects of policies on marginalized communities. The audit team also conducts interviews with stakeholders, including employees, clients, and community members to gain a deeper understanding of the impact of policies and practices

Data Collection and Review

A Civil Rights Equity Audit requires input from stakeholders. Organizations collect data in many forms to provide them with a wide range of influences that contribute to organizational achievement.

Data collection can come from a variety of sources, including:

- Listening sessions with leadership

- Observations

- Focus group interviews with board members, senior leadership, and employees

- Organizational discipline policies and code of conduct

- Information provided on the organization's website

- DEIB surveys

- Recruitment and retention reports

- Assessment data

The Benefits of Conducting a Civil Rights Equity Audit

Conducting a Civil Rights Equity Audit provides several benefits, including:

- **Promoting Equity:** The audit identifies areas of inequity and provides recommendations for addressing them. This promotes fairness, inclusivity, and equal opportunities for all individuals.

- **Enhancing Organizational Performance:** The audit provides a framework for assessing the effectiveness of policies and practices. This allows organizations to improve their performance and achieve better outcomes.

- **Legal Compliance:** The audit ensures that policies and practices align with civil rights laws and regulations. This reduces the risk of legal challenges and lawsuits.

- **Strengthening Community Relations:** The audit engages stakeholders in the process, which fosters trust and strengthens community relations. This can improve the organization's reputation and increase community support.

- **Cost Savings:** The audit can identify inefficiencies and areas where resources can be better allocated. This can result in cost savings for the organization.

A Civil Rights Equity Audit is a powerful tool for promoting equity and justice. It provides a framework for evaluating policies and practices through a lens of equity, which helps to ensure that they are fair, just, and inclusive. Conducting an audit can identify areas of inequity, promote legal compliance, enhance organizational performance, strengthen community relations, and result in cost savings. By conducting regular audits, organizations can ensure that they are upholding civil rights principles and promoting equality and justice for all.

A Civil Rights Equity Audit is very useful for looking at these practices within the organization. Organizations are responsible for making sure they are compliant with Equal Employment Opportunity Laws because it prevents lawsuits from employees and protects an organization in terms of liability. The audit will identify anywhere between three to six areas where an organization may need improvement.

The utilization of a Civil Rights Equity Audit proves to be a valuable instrument for organizations to pinpoint areas in which they may be falling short of their legal responsibilities. This examination will uncover prospects for improvement and advancement within the organization.

The benefit of conducting the Civil Rights Equity Audit is to be able to set measurable goals that the organization is able to use to support racial equity work. It enhances the organization's reputation by being transparent and accountable. It helps them be proactive to stay in compliance with their EIBD goals.

A civil rights equity audit is a specialized examination that evaluates how well an organization or institution complies with civil rights laws and promotes equitable treatment for all individuals, particularly those from marginalized groups. This audit can be conducted by various professionals and entities, depending on the scope and the specific needs of the organization.

Here are some common examples:

- **External Consultants and Firms:** Many organizations choose to hire external consultants who specialize in civil rights and EIBD strategies. These consultants are well-versed in legal compliance, organizational behavior, and cultural sensitivity. They can provide an unbiased assessment and are skilled in identifying both overt and subtle disparities in treatment.

- **Legal Experts:** Attorneys and legal experts who specialize in civil rights law can conduct these audits to ensure compliance with federal, state, and local anti-discrimination laws. Their expertise is crucial in understanding the legal framework surrounding civil rights issues within the workplace or educational institutions.

- **Academic Institutions**: Researchers or academic centers with a focus on social justice, civil rights, or equity issues may also conduct equity audits. They can bring a rigorous, research-based approach to the audit, offering both quantitative and qualitative analyses.

- **Government Agencies:** Certain government entities, such as the Equal Employment Opportunity Commission (EEOC) or the Office for Civil Rights (OCR) in educational settings, may conduct audits if there are complaints or if the organization is under review for compliance with civil rights laws.

- **Internal Teams:** Larger organizations might have internal teams dedicated to EIBD that can conduct regular equity audits. These teams, however, should operate with a level of independence to ensure objectivity in their findings.

- **Nonprofit Organizations:** Nonprofits focusing on civil rights and social justice issues might also conduct or assist in conducting equity audits, especially for other nonprofit entities or community-based organizations.

Choosing the right auditor or team of auditors often depends on the specific goals of the audit, the industry in question, and the resources available. It's important for the audit to be thorough, impartial, and aligned with the latest legal standards and best practices in civil rights and equity.

Affirmative Action Plans

Many organizations have begun implementing **Affirmative Action Plans (AAPs)**. Affirmative Action Plans are policies and programs designed to promote equal opportunities in employment, education, and other areas for historically disadvantaged groups, such as minorities and women. These plans aim to address the impact of discrimination and historical disadvantage by taking proactive steps to level the playing field and ensure that these groups have access to the same opportunities and benefits as those who have traditionally held more power and privilege.

Affirmative Action Plans are created to ensure equal employment opportunities for applicants and employees and are intended to ensure that applicants and employees have equal opportunities for recruitment, selection, and advancement without regard to their race, color, nationality, sex, sexual orientation, gender, or disability status.

Not all employers are required to have an Affirmative Action Plan; however, an employer that is receiving funding from the federal government is obligated to undertake affirmative action efforts and should have a written plan in place.

An organization should conduct an internal audit to keep track of employee demographic information and monitor anti-discrimination initiatives. The information tracked should include applicant and employee demographics, promotions, internal transfers, terminations, and compensation.

An Affirmative Action Plan will also include information about the steps that will need to be taken in order to improve representation in the workplace, as well as documented efforts of training programs and outreach efforts. These steps should be documented in the organization's personnel policies and updated annually.

History of Affirmative Action Plans

The concept of affirmative action can be traced back to the Civil Rights Act of 1964, which prohibited discrimination on the basis of race, color, religion, sex, or national origin. However, it was not until the late 1960s and early 1970s that Affirmative Action Plans began to be implemented in earnest, particularly in the areas of employment and education.

One of the first major affirmative action cases was the 1971 Supreme Court decision in Griggs v. Duke Power Co., which held that employers could be liable for discrimination even if they did not intend to discriminate if their policies or practices had a disproportionate impact on minorities. This decision paved the way for affirmative action plans that sought to address the impact of past discrimination by taking proactive steps to promote diversity and equal opportunity.

In the decades that followed, affirmative action plans became more widespread, particularly in the areas of college admissions and hiring. However, they also became more controversial, with some arguing that they were no longer necessary while others argued that they were unfair or even counterproductive.

Purpose of Affirmative Action Plans

Affirmative Action Plans are policies and programs designed to promote equal opportunities for historically disadvantaged groups. They have been the subject of controversy and debate for many years, with some arguing that they are necessary to promote equality and diversity, while others argue that they are unfair and discriminatory.

The primary purpose of AAPs is to promote equal opportunities for historically disadvantaged groups, particularly minorities, and women. Historically, these groups have been subjected to discrimination and exclusion from many areas of society, including education, employment, and housing.

Affirmative Action Plans aim to address the impact of this discrimination by taking proactive steps to promote diversity and inclusion. They may include policies such as quotas or targets for hiring or admissions, outreach programs to recruit underrepresented groups, and training programs to promote diversity and cultural competence. Proponents of AAPs argue that they are necessary to ensure that historically disadvantaged groups have access to the same opportunities and benefits as those who have traditionally held more power and privilege. They argue that without affirmative action, these groups would continue to face barriers to success and would be less likely to achieve their full potential.

Supporters of AAPs also argue that they promote diversity, which has been shown to have numerous benefits in areas such as innovation, problem-solving, and creativity. They argue that a diverse workforce or student body is better equipped to address the needs of a diverse society and to compete in a global economy.

Critics of AAPs, on the other hand, argue that they are unfair and discriminatory. They argue that AAPs give preferential treatment to certain groups based on their race or gender rather than on their qualifications or merit. They argue that this is a form of reverse discrimination that penalizes those who have worked hard and earned their positions.

Opponents of affirmative action plans also argue that they are no longer necessary, as discrimination is no longer a significant barrier to success for minorities and women. They argue that the playing field has been leveled and that affirmative action plans are now an unnecessary form of social engineering.

The U.S Supreme Court has made several significant rulings on affirmative action, particularly in the context of higher education admissions.

On June 29, 2023, the 6-3 ruling marked a significant shift in the court's stance on the use of race in college admissions. The decision to curb affirmative action ends a four-decade precedent that allowed colleges and universities to consider applicants' race as a factor in their admissions processes to promote diversity and inclusivity on campuses. With this ruling, educational institutions will face stricter limitations on the use of race-conscious admissions policies.

The specific lawsuits against Harvard University and the University of North Carolina brought the issue of racial discrimination in admissions to the forefront of the national conversation. The court's ruling may have implications for how other colleges and universities approach their admissions policies going forward.

The recent U.S. Supreme Court ruling that curbs affirmative action in higher education specifically pertains to college and university admissions processes. It does not directly impact affirmative action policies in organizations that focus on promoting diversity and inclusion in the workplace rather than college admissions.

Affirmative action in organizations involves measures taken to ensure equal employment opportunities for underrepresented groups, such as racial and ethnic minorities, women, and individuals with disabilities. These policies aim to address historical disparities and promote diversity at all levels of the workforce.

While the recent Supreme Court ruling may have implications for the discussion surrounding affirmative action and its constitutionality in different contexts, it does not alter existing affirmative action policies or practices in the corporate and business world.

It's important to recognize that affirmative action in organizations has its unique justifications and considerations, distinct from those in higher education admissions. In the workplace, diversity is often seen as a valuable asset that leads to improved decision-making, innovation, and a better understanding of diverse customer needs.

Employers remain committed to fostering an inclusive and diverse workforce, and affirmative action plays a vital role in achieving this goal. Organizations may continue to implement affirmative action initiatives to promote diversity, equity, and inclusion in their workforce in compliance with existing employment laws and guidelines.

As with any legal or policy matter, it is essential for organizations to stay informed about any changes in the legal landscape that may affect affirmative action policies. Legal experts and human resources professionals can provide guidance on navigating these matters and ensuring compliance with applicable laws and regulations.

Diversity Equity Inclusion Belonging Assessment

DEIB has become increasingly important in today's society. DEIB assessments are tools used to evaluate an organization's progress toward creating a diverse, equitable, and inclusive workplace. These assessments are an important component of an organization's DEIB strategy, as they help identify areas of improvement and allow for the development of targeted interventions.

Before crafting a DEIB Action Plan, an organization should conduct an organizational DEIB assessment. DEIB assessments can take many forms, including surveys, focus groups, interviews, and audits. The goal of these assessments is to gather information about an organization's culture, policies, and practices related to DEIB. This information can then be used to develop recommendations for improving the organization's DEIB efforts. DEIB assessments should: include staff, volunteers, and stakeholders at varying levels of the organization; focus on specific strengths and areas of growth; and be conducted in an open, judgment-free environment. They can also offer a subset of questions that examine the organization's mission, values, and goals; organizational policies and procedures; and workplace culture.

This assessment looks at the strategic factors of ensuring diversity, equity, inclusion, and belonging are built within the organization. The DEIB self-assessment is organized into eight key areas that will help your organization identify current strengths and weaknesses, areas for improvement, and action items.

DEIB assessments are designed to provide a comprehensive overview of an organization's practices related to creating a diverse and inclusive workplace. These assessments cover various key areas to ensure all aspects of DEIB are effectively addressed.

Here are eight critical areas that such assessments typically measure:

- **Recruitment and Hiring Practices:** This area evaluates whether the organization's hiring practices are designed to attract a diverse pool of candidates. It looks at the sources for recruitment, the language used in job descriptions, and the fairness and inclusivity of the screening and selection processes.

- **Employee Development and Advancement:** DEIB assessments examine if employees have equitable access to training, mentorship, and professional development opportunities that can lead to career advancement. This includes assessing promotion rates across different demographic groups to identify any patterns of disparity.

- **Workplace Culture:** This evaluates the overall environment of the workplace, including whether it supports diversity and fosters a sense of belonging. Surveys and interviews may be used to gauge employees' feelings of safety, respect, and value in their day-to-day interactions and experiences.

- **Leadership and Accountability:** Assessments look at whether leaders are committed to DEIB principles and how accountability is maintained. This involves reviewing the diversity of the leadership team and the policies in place to uphold equity and inclusion at all levels of the organization.

- **Compensation and Benefits:** This area scrutinizes the equity of compensation packages and benefits across all employee groups. It aims to uncover any pay disparities that exist along lines of race, gender, ethnicity, disability, or other categories.

- **Communication Practices:** Effective communication practices are vital for an inclusive workplace. DEIB assessments review how communication occurs within the organization, ensuring it is accessible, inclusive, and open to diverse viewpoints.

- **Policies and Procedures:** This involves a review of all organizational policies and procedures to ensure they support equity and do not inadvertently discriminate. This includes non-discrimination policies, grievance procedures, and accessibility policies.

- **Community Engagement and Impact:** Lastly, DEIB assessments often look at how the organization engages with the community and its impact on diverse groups. This includes corporate social responsibility initiatives, partnerships with minority-owned businesses, and community outreach programs.

By measuring these areas, DEIB assessments help organizations identify strengths and areas for improvement in their efforts to create a more inclusive, equitable, and supportive workplace. These insights are crucial for developing effective strategies to enhance DEIB across all aspects of the organization.

Depending on its mission, vision, and goals, each organization will define DEIB in its own way. Organizations should use this assessment as a way to examine the impact of current and future policies, procedures, services, and programs. The assessment should be used to help organizations consider their organizational culture in a broad sense while understanding how programs, policies, and decisions align with an organization's diversity, equity, inclusion, and belonging goals and outcomes.

What is the purpose of this assessment?

When completing a DEIB assessment, you want to ensure that you're building an effective DEIB strategy within the organization. It can be really difficult for the organization to know where to start and where they're going to focus their efforts. This assessment gives organizations powerful insights into the employee experience. It helps them identify where to target their efforts and resources.

The assessment aims to confirm that the organization upholds fairness and equity for all its employees. During the survey, employees express their agreement or disagreement with assessment statements, shedding light on their perceptions of respect and the availability of fair career advancement opportunities within the organization. Additionally, this assessment offers employees an opportunity to convey their feelings regarding the safety and supportiveness of the workplace environment, their comfort in discussing racial issues, and whether they have encountered any instances of microaggressions or implicit biases.

Benefits of DEIB Assessments

DEIB assessments offer several benefits to organizations. First, they provide a baseline for assessing progress toward DEIB goals. By measuring the current state of an organization's DEIB efforts, leaders can identify areas for improvement and track progress over time.

Second, DEIB assessments help identify areas of bias or discrimination within an organization. This information can be used to develop interventions aimed at reducing bias and increasing equity.

Third, DEIB assessments can improve employee engagement and retention. When employees feel that their organization values diversity, equity, inclusion, and belonging they are more likely to feel engaged and committed to their work.

Types of DEIB Assessments

There are several types of DEIB assessments that organizations can use to evaluate their DEIB efforts.

These include:

- **Surveys:** Surveys are a common tool used to gather information about an organization's DEIB efforts. They can be administered to all employees or specific groups, such as underrepresented employees or managers.

- **Focus Groups:** Focus groups are small group discussions that allow participants to share their thoughts and experiences related to DEIB. They can be used to gather in-depth information about specific topics related to DEIB.

- **Interviews:** Interviews can be conducted with employees, managers, or other stakeholders to gather information about their experiences related to DEIB. These interviews can be conducted individually or in a group setting.

- **Audits:** Audits are a systematic review of an organization's policies, procedures, and practices related to DEIB. They can be conducted by internal or external auditors and can provide a comprehensive review of an organization's DEIB efforts.

Data Collection and Review

A DEIB assessment requires input from employees. Organizations collect data in many forms to provide them with a wide range of influences that contribute to organizational achievement.

Data collection can come from a variety of sources, including:

- Inclusion Climate Survey

- Reflective dialogue

- Focus group interviews with board members, senior leadership, and employees

- Organizational policies and procedures

- Information provided on the organization's website

Conducting a DEIB Assessment

When conducting a DEIB assessment, it is important to follow a systematic process to ensure that the assessment is comprehensive and effective.

The following steps can be taken to conduct a DEIB assessment:

- **Define the scope:** The first step in conducting a DEIB assessment is to define the scope of the assessment. This includes identifying the goals of the assessment, the areas to be assessed, and the stakeholders to be involved.

- **Develop assessment tools:** Once the scope has been defined, the next step is to develop the assessment tools. This may include surveys, focus group scripts, interview guides, or audit checklists.

- **Collect data:** The data collection phase involves administering assessment tools to gather information about the organization's DEIB efforts. This may involve administering surveys, conducting focus groups or interviews, or conducting an audit.

- **Analyze data:** Once the data has been collected, it must be analyzed to identify patterns and themes. This analysis can be done qualitatively or quantitatively, depending on the type of data collected.

- **Develop recommendations:** Based on the data analysis, recommendations can be developed to improve the organization's DEIB efforts. These recommendations should be specific, measurable, achievable, relevant, and time-bound (SMART).

- **Implement recommendations:** The final step in conducting a DEIB assessment is to implement the recommendations. This may involve revising policies and procedures, providing training and development opportunities, or making changes to the organization's culture.

Challenges and Best Practices

Conducting DEIB assessments can pose significant challenges, especially in cases where an organization is hesitant to embrace change. These challenges often manifest in various forms. One common hurdle is encountering resistance to altering existing policies, procedures, or the prevailing organizational culture, even when the assessment uncovers areas warranting improvement. Another obstacle can be the scarcity of essential resources—DEIB assessments demand significant investments in terms of time, finances, and available resources, which can be limited in certain organizations. Additionally, securing the commitment and support of critical stakeholders, such as senior leadership, managers, and employees, is imperative for the success of a DEIB assessment.

Despite these challenges, there are several best practices that organizations can follow to ensure that their DEIB assessments are effective:

- **Involve key stakeholders:** It is important to involve key stakeholders in the assessment process to ensure buy-in and support.

- **Use multiple assessment tools:** Using multiple assessment tools, such as surveys, focus groups, and audits, can provide a more comprehensive view of an organization's DEIB efforts.

- **Ensure confidentiality:** It is important to ensure that the data collected during the assessment process is kept confidential to encourage honest and open sharing.

- **Use a third-party facilitator:** In some cases, it may be beneficial to use a third-party facilitator to conduct the assessment, particularly if there are concerns about the objectivity of internal staff.

- **Develop a clear action plan:** Developing a clear action plan based on the assessment results can help ensure that the organization makes progress toward its DEIB goals.

- **Communicate the results:** Communicating the results of the assessment to key stakeholders is important to ensure that everyone is aware of the organization's DEIB strengths and weaknesses.

DEIB assessments are an important tool for organizations looking to create a more diverse, equitable, and inclusive workplace. By identifying areas of improvement and developing targeted interventions, organizations can make progress toward their DEIB goals. While conducting a DEIB assessment can be challenging, following best practices, and involving key stakeholders can help ensure that the assessment is effective and leads to meaningful change.

Organizations that are working towards diversity, equity, inclusion, and belonging are often confused about which assessment would be the most beneficial.

Organizations need to decide which assessment they need to do based on their organizational goals and what outcomes they want to be measured. It is possible that an organization may choose to conduct both a Civil Rights Equity Audit and DEIB assessment. Each tool has its own benefits and is very different in its approach.

As organizations strive to build a more equitable and inclusive environment, understanding the distinctions between DEIB assessment and Civil Rights Equity Audit is vital. By recognizing their respective scopes, objectives, and shared indicators, organizations can bridge the gap and develop a more comprehensive approach to equity evaluation. Leveraging both frameworks empowers organizations to navigate complex equity challenges, fosters a culture of inclusivity, and drives positive change toward a more equitable workplace and society.

Case Study

Civil Rights Equity Audit of the Minneapolis Police Department

In 2020, following the murder of George Floyd, the Minneapolis City Council and the Minnesota Department of Human Rights launched a civil rights equity audit of the Minneapolis Police Department (MPD). The audit was designed to assess the department's policies, practices, and procedures related to race and gender equity and to identify areas for improvement.

The audit was conducted by a team of independent evaluators with expertise in civil rights and law enforcement and included a review of data and documents, interviews with MPD staff, and engagement with community members and stakeholders.

The audit identified a number of areas where the MPD was not meeting its obligations under civil rights law, including:

- Disproportionate use of force against people of color, particularly African Americans.

- Lack of accountability for officers who engage in misconduct.

- Racial profiling and bias in policing practices.

- Insufficient diversity and cultural competency among MPD staff.

The audit also identified a number of recommendations for improving equity and accountability within the department, including:

- Requiring officers to intervene and report when they witness excessive force or other forms of misconduct.

- Implementing a system for tracking and addressing patterns of misconduct.

- Enhancing community engagement and input in the development of MPD policies and procedures.

- Increasing diversity and cultural competency training for MPD staff.

- Reevaluating the role of police in responding to non-violent calls for service, such as mental health crises and minor traffic violations.

The results of the civil rights equity audit were used to inform ongoing efforts to reform the MPD, including the development of a new community-led public safety model, the creation of a Department of Community Safety and Violence Prevention, and the implementation of new policies and procedures aimed at improving equity and accountability within the department.

The Minneapolis Police Department's civil rights equity audit is an important example of how equity audits can help identify areas of improvement and inform ongoing efforts to promote civil rights and social justice within public institutions. The audit helped to shine a spotlight on longstanding issues of racial bias and misconduct within the MPD and provided a roadmap for meaningful reform and change.

Integrative Exercise

DEIB Assessment Challenge

DEIB Assessment Challenge is a game designed to help participants understand the importance of DEIB assessments in the workplace. It is a team-based game that requires critical thinking, problem-solving, and communication skills.

The objective of the game is to help participants understand the importance of DEIB assessments, identify potential DEIB issues in the workplace, and develop strategies to address those issues. The game can be played in a 60-90 minute session. The game can be played by 4-6 players per team.

Materials

- Flipchart paper

- Markers

- Sticky notes

- DEIB assessment templates (created ahead of time)

Step 1: Introduce the game and form teams

The facilitator introduces the game and divides the participants into teams of 4-6 people. Each team is given a set of materials.

Step 2: Explain the DEIB Assessment

The facilitator explains the concept of DEIB assessments, including what they are, why they are important, and how they are conducted.

Step 3: Assign roles

Each team member is assigned a role, such as a facilitator, note-taker, timekeeper, and presenter.

Step 4: Analyze the DEI Assessment Templates

Each team is given a set of DEIB assessment templates that have been created ahead of time. The templates contain scenarios and questions related to DEIB issues in the workplace.

Step 5: Brainstorm Solutions

Teams analyze the templates and brainstorm potential solutions to the DEIB issues. They write their ideas on sticky notes and place them on the flipchart paper.

Step 6: Present Solutions

Each team presents their solutions to the group. The facilitator leads a discussion on the pros and cons of each solution.

Step 7: Evaluate the Solutions

Teams evaluate the solutions presented by other teams and provide feedback. They discuss which solutions are the most effective and why.

Step 8: Debrief

The facilitator leads a debrief session to discuss what was learned from the game, including the importance of DEIB assessments, how to identify potential DEIB issues in the workplace, and how to develop effective strategies to address those issues.

The DEIB Assessment Challenge is a fun and interactive way to help participants understand the importance of DEIB assessments and develop strategies to address potential issues in the workplace. Through the game, participants are encouraged to think critically and work collaboratively to come up with effective solutions. The game also provides an opportunity for participants to learn from each other and share their perspectives on DEIB issues.

The DEIB Assessment Challenge can be customized to suit the needs and goals of different organizations. The facilitator can modify the templates to include scenarios and questions that are relevant to the organization's specific DEIB challenges.

Overall, the DEIB Assessment Challenge is a valuable tool for organizations that are committed to building a more inclusive and equitable workplace. By engaging employees in a fun and interactive way, the game can help foster a culture of DEIB and promote meaningful change in the organization.

Chapter Four

Building a Dynamic EIBD Committee

E IBD committees are essential components of any organization that values diversity and strives to create an inclusive culture. These committees are responsible for developing and implementing strategies that promote diversity, equity, and inclusion in the workplace.

A EIBD Committee is a group of individuals who work within the organization from different departments and take the lead and initiative on the organization's EIBD journey. They plan, promote, strategize, and educate the organization's diversity, equity, inclusion, and belonging mission and vision within the workplace. In this chapter, we will explore the role of EIBD committees, their benefits, and how they can help organizations create a culture of belonging.

What are EIBD Committees?

EIBD committees, which stand for Equity, Inclusion, Belonging, and Diversity committees, are groups within organizations dedicated to advancing and overseeing initiatives that foster a more equitable, inclusive, and diverse workplace. These committees are tasked with developing, implementing, and monitoring policies, programs, and practices that support the EIBD framework. They are usually formed by the organization's leadership and comprise representatives from different departments or employee resource groups (ERGs). The committees are responsible for developing and implementing strategies that promote EIBD in the workplace. They work to create an inclusive culture where all employees feel valued, respected, and supported.

Benefits of EIBD Committees

EIBD committees offer numerous benefits to organizations. First, they help create a culture of belonging where employees feel valued and supported. This leads to increased employee engagement, higher job satisfaction, and reduced turnover rates. Second, EIBD committees help organizations attract and retain diverse talent. By promoting EIBD, organizations can attract a wider pool of job candidates and create a more equitable workforce. Third, EIBD committees help organizations improve performance and innovation. Diverse teams are more likely to generate innovative solutions, which can lead to increased productivity and revenue.

How EIBD Committees Can Help Organizations Create a Culture of Belonging

EIBD committees can help organizations create a culture of belonging in several ways. First, they can develop and implement training programs that promote EIBD. These programs can help employees understand the importance of equity and how to create an inclusive workplace. Second, EIBD committees can create and promote employee resource groups (ERGs). ERGs are voluntary, employee-led groups that provide support, networking, and professional development opportunities to members who share a common identity or interest. ERGs can help employees feel valued, supported, and connected to their colleagues. Third, EIBD committees can develop and implement policies and procedures that promote equity, inclusion, belonging, and diversity. For example, they can ensure the job postings use inclusive language and that hiring practices are fair and unbiased.

The EIBD Committee should create a checklist for forming and sustaining the committee. This checklist should identify whether or not the organization has conducted an Equity or DEIB assessment previously. It should include the committee's purpose and mission statements, identify the various roles within the committee, and address the goals and measurable outcomes that the committee wants to achieve.

The committee should include a communication plan for how they will communicate the progress to the key members of the organization; senior leadership, the board, and the employees of the organization.

Recruiting Members and Duties

Before recruiting members for a EIBD committee, it is important to define the purpose and goals of the committee. This will help to attract individuals who are passionate about EIBD and have the necessary skills and experience to contribute to the committee's work. The purpose of the committee should be clearly stated in the job description and communicated during the recruitment process.

EIBD committees require a diverse range of skills and experience. Members should have a deep understanding of EIBD issues and a passion for promoting equality and inclusivity within the workplace. They should also have strong communication and interpersonal skills, as well as the ability to work collaboratively with others. Additionally, members with expertise in areas such as human resources, legal, and communications can bring valuable insights to the committee.

Some questions organizations can ask themselves when recruiting members include:

- Do the people who want to become members have a passion for EIBD work?

- Do they have lived experience?

- Are they going to be committed to this work and be accountable?

- Are they open to learning, are they able to communicate well?

- Do the members have diverse backgrounds?

A successful EIBD committee should be diverse and inclusive. This means recruiting members from a range of backgrounds, including different ethnicities, genders, ages, and abilities. Additionally, it is important to ensure that the recruitment process is free from bias and discrimination and that all candidates are given equal consideration.

The recruitment process should be open and transparent to ensure that a diverse range of candidates is attracted. Promoting the opportunity widely through job boards, social media, and employee networks can help to reach a broad range of potential candidates. Additionally, it is important to ensure that the job description and application process are accessible to all candidates, including those with disabilities. Employees should be encouraged to self-nominate or nominate colleagues for the EIBD committee. This can help to identify individuals who are passionate about EIBD and have the necessary skills and experience to contribute to the committee's work. Employee nominations can also help to ensure that the committee is representative of the wider workforce.

Term limits are essential, aiming to bring in fresh voices to the committee, with the objective of allowing new members to join. The optimal term duration should not exceed three years, and members can reapply after completing their term. The primary aim should be to continually rejuvenate the committee, fostering opportunities for innovative perspectives to emerge.

The EIBD Committee members are ambassadors for equity, inclusion, belonging, and diversity. Their role is to build a business case for the EIBD efforts across the organization. They work with the training department and human resources department to identify specific EIBD training and workshops that are needed internally. They also collaborate with the human resources department to mediate employee experiences of discrimination or racial bias. They are the ones who will be resources to assist during recruitment and hiring, as well as examining organizational policies and procedures through an equity lens and making recommendations for changes that need to be implemented in regard to equity, inclusion, belonging, and diversity. They also work with the communications team by creating content to be delivered to every employee, possibly in the form of a newsletter or mass email to announce scheduled upcoming EIBD workshops and events.

Members should make themselves accessible for the purpose of recognizing and tackling emerging issues that affect EIBD initiatives within the organization. Participation in this committee should be an enjoyable experience. The onboarding process should be a pleasant opportunity to connect with new members, inquire about their motivations for engaging in this work, learn about their upbringing, and understand how their background has shaped their perspectives. You should also explore what factors have inspired their interest and passion for EIBD work.

Recruiting the right members for a EIBD committee is crucial to the success of the committee and its ability to drive EIBD initiatives within the organization. By defining the purpose of the committee, identifying the key skills and experience needed, promoting the opportunity widely, encouraging employee nominations, and ensuring diversity and inclusion, organizations can attract a diverse range of passionate individuals who can contribute to the committee's work. It is also important to provide ongoing support and training for committee members to ensure they have the necessary skills and knowledge to drive EIBD initiatives effectively. Ultimately, a successful EIBD committee can play a critical role in creating a more inclusive and equitable workplace culture, benefiting both employees and the organization as a whole.

Challenges of EIBD Committees

EIBD committees face several challenges that can hinder their effectiveness. One of the biggest challenges is resistance from some employees who may not understand or value EIBD. This can lead to a lack of participation in EIBD initiatives, which could undermine the committee's efforts. Additionally, EIBD committees may face challenges in collecting and analyzing data on equity and inclusion in the workplace. This can make it difficult to identify areas for improvement or measure the impact of EIBD initiatives.

Another challenge that EIBD committees may face is a lack of resources, both in terms of time and funding. EIBD initiatives often require significant resources to implement effectively, and committees may need to compete with other priorities for these resources. Finally, EIBD committees may face challenges in ensuring that their initiatives are sustainable over the long term. It is essential to embed EIBD into the organization's culture and values rather than treating it as a one-time initiative.

Best Practices for EIBD Committees

To overcome these challenges, EIBD committees can follow best practices that promote inclusivity and effectiveness. First, it is essential to involve employees from all levels and departments in the committee's work. This can help ensure that the committee's initiatives are relevant and actionable across the organization. Second, EIBD committees should establish clear goals and metrics to measure success. This can help ensure that the committee's efforts are focused and effective. Third, EIBD committees should prioritize transparency and communication with all employees. This can help build trust and engagement in the committee's initiatives.

EIBD committees are essential components of any organization that values diversity and strives to create an inclusive culture. By promoting

EIBD, committees can help organizations create a culture of belonging where all employees feel valued, respected, and supported. While there are challenges to implementing EIBD initiatives, following best practices can help ensure that the committee's efforts are effective and sustainable over the long term.

Case Study

Forming a EIBD Committee

A mid-sized company with approximately 500 employees. The company's leadership team has recognized the importance of EIBD and wants to establish a EIBD committee to ensure that the company is taking proactive steps to promote a more diverse and inclusive workplace.

Step 1: Determine the Purpose and Scope of the EIBD Committee

The first step in forming a EIBD committee is to determine the purpose and scope of the committee.

The leadership team decided that the committee's purpose would be to:

- Ensure that the company's policies, practices, and procedures promote diversity, equity, inclusion, and belonging.

- Promote a culture of inclusion and respect for all employees.

- Identify and address any barriers to diversity and inclusion within the company.

- Develop and implement initiatives to attract, retain, and promote diverse talent.

- Foster partnerships with external organizations that can help the company achieve its EIBD goals.

Step 2: Identify Committee Members

The second step in forming a EIBD committee is to identify committee members. The committee was composed of a cross-functional group of employees, including representatives from human resources, operations, marketing, and finance. The company also ensured that the committee was diverse in terms of gender, race, ethnicity, age, and other characteristics.

Step 3: Establish Clear Roles and Responsibilities

The third step in forming a EIBD committee is to establish clear roles and responsibilities for committee members.

The committee was responsible for:

- Developing and implementing a EIBD plan for the company.

- Conducting regular assessments of the company's EIBD initiatives.

- Providing recommendations to the leadership team on how to improve EIBD efforts.

- Communicating progress and updates on EIBD initiatives to all employees.

Step 4: Provide Training and Resources

The fourth step in forming a EIBD committee is to provide training and resources to committee members to ensure that they have the knowledge and skills needed to carry out their roles effectively. The company provided committee members with resources such as EIBD toolkits, training on unconscious bias, and access to external consultants and experts in EIBD.

Step 5: Establish Metrics and Reporting

The fifth step in forming a EIBD committee is to establish metrics and reporting mechanisms to track progress toward EIBD goals. The company established metrics such as employee demographics, employee engagement, and turnover rates to track progress toward EIBD goals. The committee was responsible for collecting and analyzing the data and reporting progress to the leadership team.

In conclusion, forming a EIBD committee requires careful planning and execution. By following these steps, the company was able to establish a EIBD committee that was well-equipped to promote diversity, equity, inclusion, and belonging within the company.

Integrative Exercise

EIBD Committee Checklist

EIBD Committee Checklist Suggestions to Consider:

- The executives of the organization approve and desire the work of EIBD and have appointed a committee for oversight.

- A clear mission and vision statement has been defined for the committee that aligns with the organization's EIBD goals.

- The committee has diverse representation.

- Specific, measurable, and time-bound goals for EIBD initiatives have been established.

- Key objectives to track progress and success have been outlined.

- Action plans for addressing EIBD issues within the organization have been developed.

- Actionable steps and responsible parties for each initiative have been identified.

- EIBD training and educational sessions for committee members and employees have been scheduled.

- A communication strategy to keep the organization informed about EIBD efforts has been developed.

- Employees and stakeholders have been engaged to gather feedback and promote transparency.

- Key performance indicators (KPIs) to measure EIBD progress have been established.

- Data related to diversity and inclusion within the organization has been collected and analyzed.

- Programs and policies to promote inclusivity and reduce bias have been implemented.

- Opportunities for the organization to engage with the broader community on EIBD matters have been explored.

- Mechanisms for employees to provide feedback and share concerns have been created.

- Regular evaluations of the committee's effectiveness are conducted and strategies are adjusted as needed.

- Necessary resources are allocated to support EIBD initiatives and activities.

- A feedback loop with senior leadership to ensure alignment with the organization's overall strategy has been established.

- Success stories and case studies have been shared to inspire others and showcase the positive impact of EIBD work.

- Strategies to ensure the sustainability of EIBD efforts over the long term have been developed.

- The EIBD committee checklist is periodically reviewed and updated to adapt to evolving needs and priorities.

Chapter Five

History of Marginalized Groups and Discrimination in the Workplace

The history of marginalized groups and discrimination in the workplace is a long and complex one, stretching back centuries. Throughout history, various groups have been marginalized and discriminated against in the workplace, including women, people of color, LGBTQ+ individuals, and people with disabilities. This chapter will explore the history of discrimination in the workplace against these groups, examining the various forms it has taken over time, and the efforts that have been made to address it.

Women in the Workplace

Discrimination against women in the workplace has been a common practice throughout history. In the 19th century, women were largely excluded from the workforce, with their traditional role being seen as that of a homemaker and caregiver. However, as the 20th century dawned, women began to enter the workforce in increasing numbers, often taking on low-paying, low-status jobs.

Despite this progress, women continued to face discrimination in the workplace. Women were often paid less than men for doing the same work and were frequently passed over for promotions and other opportunities for advancement. Sexual harassment was also a pervasive problem, with male colleagues and superiors often taking advantage of their power in order to make unwelcome advances or engage in other forms of inappropriate behavior.

In recent decades, there have been efforts to address these issues through legislation such as the Equal Pay Act of 1963, the Civil Rights Act of 1964, and the Pregnancy Discrimination Act of 1978. However, despite these efforts, women continue to face discrimination in the workplace today, with the gender pay gap and sexual harassment remaining persistent problems.

People of Color in the Workplace

People of color have also faced significant discrimination in the workplace throughout history. In the United States, racial discrimination in the workplace was legalized for much of the country's history, with laws such as Jim Crow and segregation policies keeping people of color in low-paying, menial jobs.

Even after the Civil Rights Act of 1964 was passed, people of color continued to face discrimination in the workplace. They were often paid less than their white counterparts and were frequently passed over for promotions and other opportunities for advancement. Racial slurs and other forms of harassment were also common, creating a hostile work environment for people of color.

Efforts to address racial discrimination in the workplace have included affirmative action policies, which aim to increase diversity in the workplace by giving preference to underrepresented groups in hiring and promotion decisions. However, as discussed in chapter three, affirmative action remains a controversial issue, with some arguing that it unfairly favors certain groups over others.

LGBTQ+ Individuals in the Workplace

Discrimination against LGBTQ+ individuals in the workplace is a relatively recent phenomenon, as societal attitudes towards homosexuality and other forms of non-heteronormative behavior have shifted over time. In the past, being openly LGBTQ+ was often grounds for dismissal from one's job, and many LGBTQ+ individuals were forced to hide their identities in order to avoid discrimination and harassment.

In recent years, there have been efforts to address discrimination against LGBTQ+ individuals in the workplace. In 2020, the U.S. Supreme Court ruled that discrimination based on sexual orientation or gender identity is illegal under Title VII of the Civil Rights Act of 1964. However, despite this ruling, discrimination against LGBTQ+ individuals remains a problem in many workplaces, and many LGBTQ+ individuals continue to face harassment and discrimination on the job.

People with Disabilities in the Workplace

People with disabilities have also faced discrimination in the workplace throughout history. In the past, people with disabilities were often excluded from the workforce altogether, with their conditions being seen as a liability or hindrance to their ability to work. Those who were able to find employment often faced discriminatory attitudes and policies, such as being paid less for doing the same work as their non-disabled colleagues.

In recent years, there have been efforts to address discrimination against people with disabilities in the workplace. The Americans with Disabilities Act (ADA), passed in 1990, prohibits discrimination against individuals with disabilities in all aspects of employment, including hiring, firing, and promotion decisions. The law also requires employers to provide reasonable accommodations to employees with disabilities, such as modified work schedules or assistive technology.

Despite these legal protections, people with disabilities continue to face discrimination in the workplace. They are often passed over for job opportunities or given menial tasks and may face negative attitudes from employers and colleagues.

Social Identity Discrimination

Social identity discrimination in the workplace refers to the unfair treatment of individuals based on their membership in a particular social group, such as race, gender, sexual orientation, religion, or disability status. This type of discrimination can take many forms, including harassment, exclusion, bias in hiring or promotion decisions, and pay inequities.

One of the most common forms of social identity discrimination in the workplace is racial discrimination. People of color are often subjected to negative stereotypes and biases that can lead to unfair treatment, such as being passed over for job opportunities or promotions, receiving lower pay or being subjected to hostile work environments. Similarly, women, LGBTQ+ individuals, people with disabilities, and members of other marginalized groups can also face discrimination and bias in the workplace.

Social identity discrimination can have serious negative consequences for individuals, including reduced job satisfaction, lower self-esteem, and decreased productivity. It can also have a broader impact on society, contributing to income inequality, reduced economic growth, and social unrest.

Social identity is like a unique puzzle. Specific identities make up the puzzle pieces. The term intersectionality refers to the way in which these social identities can overlap. Intersectionality creates overlapping and interdependent systems of discrimination or disadvantage.

While looking through the list of social identities (race, age, sexual orientation, immigration status, gender, ability, religion, and class), you may have struggled to answer exactly how you identify. It's normal to have more knowledge and experience with certain social identities over others. It's important for individuals to take the time to examine their own social identities, how they perceive themselves and how others perceive them, how these identities shaped their worldview and experience, and how their identities interact with each other. This practice is important for everyone because our understanding of social identities can change over time. Identity plays a large part in how we move through the world and, therefore, how people systems treat us and the opportunities that are available to us.

Each of the social identities listed above create systems of advantage and oppression that are present in the United States. There are policies and practices that are ingrained in our daily lives that benefit people of certain social identities over others, thereby maintaining the power held by those who are considered to have privileged identities.

Social identity is at the root of how we as individuals experience the world. We do not shut down our social identities when we enter the workplace. Instead, they are informed about how we work together and often determine who has access to power within the organization. For that reason, it is crucial to take time to ensure all employees have an understanding of social identities and their relation to power and privilege.

There are several strategies that employers can use to address social identity discrimination in the workplace. One important step is to create a culture of inclusivity and respect, where all employees are valued and treated fairly, regardless of their background or identity. This can be achieved through training programs, diversity and inclusion initiatives, and clear policies against discrimination and harassment.

Another important strategy is to ensure that hiring and promotion decisions are made fairly and based on merit, rather than on biases or stereotypes. This can be achieved by implementing objective criteria for evaluating job candidates, such as skills assessments, and by using diverse hiring panels to prevent groupthink and bias.

Finally, it is important for employers to take complaints of discrimination seriously and to act quickly to address any instances of bias or harassment in the workplace. This can help to create a safe and inclusive work environment where all employees feel valued and respected.

After creating a shared understanding, organizations can provide space for employees to speak about how their personal social identities impact how they work, including their relationships with their colleagues and organizational policies. By providing spaces to speak about identity, organizations can work to determine whether their policies and practices are equitable, such as whether social identity affects employees' pay or access to promotions. It also affects whether an employee feels comfortable bringing their authentic self into the workplace and feels that their expression of each of their social identities will be welcomed, respected, supported, and valued.

Systemic Inequality in Corporate Culture

When systemic inequality is present in the corporate culture, Black employees report feeling less supported, engaged, and dedicated to their employers than their non-Black co-workers. Many employers create diversity and inclusion programs to help improve the day-to-day experience of employees; however, many initiatives often fall short. The problem with many DEIB programs is that they tend to focus on helping employees from marginalized and underrepresented groups fit into the status quo company culture, rather than taking action to remove systemic barriers to equality within their organizations.

Organizations can start by leveraging data analytics to assess whether employees feel included in their teams and if they're being treated equitably within the organization at large. In collecting information about the diversity of their workforce, employers should refer to EEO data collected for compliance and obligations. Once data is collected, it should be compared to the data available on the labor market, and employers should look for gaps in diversity and draft a plan to hire and retain more members of underrepresented groups.

Being a marginalized employee in the workplace can be emotionally taxing. Creating Employee Resource Groups (ERG) is an approach that organizations can use to build a more inclusive environment and address diversity and inclusion in a more holistic, community-based way. ERGs can empower underrepresented groups by giving each group ways to discuss issues with decision-makers and leadership. ERGs support learning and development by offering formal and informal leadership opportunities and creating visibility for employees who are active.

An ERG provides resources and guidance for corporate leadership regarding diversity issues, community needs, and policy. An employer should assess how much of their workforce of marginalized employees feel comfortable bringing themselves into the workplace.

The history of marginalized groups and discrimination in the workplace is a long and complex one, with many different groups facing discrimination and marginalization over time. While there have been efforts to address these issues through legislation and advocacy, discrimination in the workplace remains a persistent problem for many individuals today. It is important for employers and policymakers to continue working towards creating a more equitable and inclusive workplace for all individuals, regardless of their race, gender, sexual orientation, disability status, or other characteristics.

Case Study

Rosie the Riveter

One notable case study for the history of marginalized groups and discrimination in the workplace is the story of the "Rosie the Riveter" campaign during World War II.

During the war, many men were drafted to fight overseas, leaving a significant labor shortage in the United States. To fill the gap, the government launched a "Rosie the Riveter" campaign to encourage women to join the workforce, particularly in the manufacturing and defense industries.

These women became known as "Rosies" and they played a critical role in the war effort by building planes, ships, and other essential equipment. However, despite their contributions, they faced discrimination and marginalization in the workplace.

Many of the women who joined the workforce were from marginalized groups, including women of color, low-income women, and women with disabilities. They were often paid less than their male counterparts and given the most menial and dangerous jobs.

Additionally, these women faced harassment and discrimination on the job. They were sometimes subjected to sexual harassment and verbal abuse, and many were told that they were taking jobs away from men who were fighting in the war.

Despite these challenges, the "Rosies" persevered and helped to pave the way for future generations of women in the workforce. Their fight for equal pay and fair treatment in the workplace helped to lay the foundation for modern labor laws and workplace protections.

Integrative Exercise

Exploring the History of Marginalized Groups and Discrimination in the Workplace

One integrative exercise for exploring the history of marginalized groups and discrimination in the workplace is to engage in a group discussion and analysis of relevant case studies.

Step 1: Forms Small Groups

Divide participants into small groups and provide each group with a case study that illustrates discrimination or marginalization in the workplace. Case studies could include historic examples such as the Montgomery Bus Boycott or contemporary examples such as the Google pay discrimination lawsuit.

Step 2: Read and Analyze Case Studies

Have each group read and analyze their case study, identifying key themes and issues related to discrimination and marginalization in the workplace.

Step 3: Gather and Discuss

Bring the groups back together and have each group present their case study and analysis to the larger group. Encourage participants to ask questions and engage in discussion about the themes and issues that emerge.

Step 4: Identify Patterns and Root Causes

Facilitate a group discussion that synthesizes the themes and issues that emerged from the case studies. Encourage participants to identify patterns and connections between the different cases, and to discuss the root causes of discrimination and marginalization in the workplace.

Step 5: Brainstorm Strategies

Finally, brainstorm strategies for addressing discrimination and promoting inclusion in the workplace. Encourage participants to think creatively and consider both individual and systemic approaches.

By engaging in this exercise, participants can deepen their understanding of the history of marginalized groups and discrimination in the workplace, and work together to identify strategies for creating more inclusive and equitable workplaces.

Chapter Six

Tackling Unconscious Bias for Lasting Change

In this chapter, we will discuss the importance of recognizing biases and discovering new ways of managing them to drive a better outcome for organizations. Much of this is related to how we learn, so let's begin with the four stages of learning.

When we learn anything, we progress through these four stages. The learning process can often be more difficult than necessary because of the negative feeling people get when they make a mistake. A proper understanding of the stages of learning can help people focus on learning new skills and proper techniques.

The Four Stages of Learning

The four stages of learning, often referred to as the **"Four Stages of Competence"** or **"Conscious Competence Model,"** were developed by Martin M. Broadwell. These stages describe the process of acquiring a new skill or competence. The initial phase of the learning process is known as **"Unconscious Incompetence."** During this stage, learners lack awareness of the skills or knowledge they require. They may not even recognize their shortcomings or the need for improvement. To illustrate this stage within the context of beginning a new job, consider the scenario where you're enthusiastic about starting a new position, but you are unaware of the systems or processes necessary to fulfill your job responsibilities.

The second phase of the learning process is termed **"Conscious Incompetence."** During this stage, learners become cognizant of their deficiency in skills or knowledge. They may encounter challenges while trying to acquire the new skill, finding it difficult to execute correctly. To extend the analogy to a new job situation, this stage corresponds to the moment when you become aware of the necessary concepts and ideas. For instance, on your first day of training, you watch a video explaining the key concepts required for success in your role. However, you still lack the ability to independently perform the job tasks.

The third phase of learning is referred to as **"Conscious Competence."** During this stage, the learner has acquired skills or knowledge through practice and focused effort. They can execute the skill correctly, but it still demands deliberate attention and concentration. In the context of your new job, this stage involves the active implementation of the acquired concepts. You're starting to gain confidence and proficiency, enabling you to handle certain tasks independently. However, you continue to engage with your supervisor frequently throughout the day to seek clarification on job-related aspects. Your work pace remains deliberate, and you may refer to training materials to assist you with your duties.

The fourth and ultimate stage of learning is **"Unconscious Competence."** In this concluding stage, the skill or knowledge has become ingrained in the learner. They can execute the skill effortlessly, without the need for conscious deliberation. In the context of your new job, you've become so adept that you can carry out tasks almost automatically. There's little need for concentrated effort or constantly determining what to do next because your job has become a well-established routine.

It is important to note that these stages are not always linear or sequential, and some learners may move back and forth between stages depending on the situation or context. However, understanding these stages can help learners and educators plan and adjust their approach to learning and teaching.

Realizing the Importance of Recognizing Biases

As an organization realizes the importance of recognizing biases, they will want to manage them to drive better operational outcomes.

Let's explore how biases work in our minds.

Biases are inherent in human beings, and they can significantly impact our decision-making processes. Recognizing biases is crucial because it allows us to make objective decisions based on facts rather than our preconceptions. Biases can lead to errors in judgment, misunderstanding, and discrimination, which can cause harm to individuals and society as a whole. In this chapter, we will explore the importance of recognizing biases and how this can help us make better decisions.

According to Barb Taylor, author of *The Biology Behind Bias*, addressing personality differences presents not just a psychological challenge but also a biological one. Our unconscious brain, shaped by evolution, has a natural inclination to favor individuals who resemble us, regardless of our conscious intentions. These similarities can encompass physical attributes, abilities, gender, race, socio-economic status, sexual orientation, or identity—attributes that ideally should not impact workplace dynamics. Additionally, they can extend to personality distinctions, such as confidence, willingness to take risks, orientation, and other factors that influence behaviors and traits critical to job effectiveness.

Biases are often formed by our experiences, beliefs, and cultural backgrounds. They can be conscious or unconscious, and they can manifest in various forms. For example, **confirmation bias** occurs when we seek out information that confirms our pre-existing beliefs and ignore information that contradicts them. Similarly, the **halo effect** occurs when we attribute positive qualities to someone based on one favorable characteristic, whereas the **horn effect** occurs when we ascribe negative qualities to someone based solely on one unfavorable characteristic. These biases can significantly impact our decision-making, and it is essential to recognize them to make objective decisions.

Daniel Kahneman published a book in 2011 entitled *Thinking Fast and Slow*. It expresses how two systems in the brain are constantly fighting over control of our behavior and actions. The author shares the many ways in which this leads to errors in memory, judgment, and decisions. System one thinking occurs in the back of the brain. It's reactive and never turns off. It is automatic. System two thinking occurs in the pre-frontal neocortex, the rational, conscious part of the brain.

Sigmund Freud held the belief that behavior and personality arise from the continuous and distinctive interplay of conflicting psychological forces functioning at three distinct levels of consciousness: the preconscious, conscious, and unconscious. He was of the opinion that each of these aspects of the mind exerts a significant influence on one's behavior.

According to Freud's psychoanalytic theory of the mind, the preconscious mind is the part of the mind that contains information that is not currently in awareness but can be readily recalled and brought into conscious awareness. It includes memories, thoughts, and feelings that are not at the forefront of consciousness but can be easily accessed with little effort.

The preconscious mind is situated between the unconscious mind, which contains repressed and inaccessible memories and desires, and the conscious mind, which is the awareness of one's immediate surroundings and mental processes. The preconscious mind can be seen as a "buffer zone" between the unconscious and conscious minds, serving as a gateway for information to move between the two.

One of Freud's key ideas was that the preconscious mind played a crucial role in the formation of personality and behavior. He believed that the preconscious mind was responsible for the filtering and processing of external stimuli and that it played a major role in decision-making and problem-solving.

For example, when faced with a difficult decision, the preconscious mind may draw on past experiences and memories to help the individual make the best choice. Similarly, the preconscious mind can influence behavior by bringing to awareness previously repressed material, which can then be analyzed and worked through in therapy.

The conscious mind is the part of the mind that is responsible for an individual's immediate awareness of their surroundings and mental processes. It includes thoughts, feelings, perceptions, and memories that are currently in awareness.

According to Freud's psychoanalytic theory, the conscious mind is the most superficial level of mental activity, and it is only a small fraction of the total mental activity that takes place in the human mind. However, while the conscious mind may be limited in its capacity, it is still an essential part of an individual's mental life, and it plays a crucial role in shaping behavior and personality.

The conscious mind is responsible for many important functions, including perception, attention, memory, and reasoning. It allows individuals to interact with their environment, make decisions, and respond to situations in a timely and appropriate manner. For example, when someone is driving a car, their conscious mind is responsible for processing information from the road, making decisions about speed and direction, and responding to changes in traffic.

In addition to its practical functions, the conscious mind is also central to an individual's sense of self. It is responsible for creating a sense of continuity and coherence in an individual's thoughts and actions, allowing them to form a stable and consistent sense of identity over time.

Overall, the conscious mind is an essential component of human mental life, and it plays a critical role in shaping behavior, personality, and the overall experience of being human.

The unconscious mind is a term used in psychoanalytic theory to describe a part of the mind that operates outside of conscious awareness. According to this theory, the unconscious mind contains thoughts, feelings, memories, and desires that are not readily accessible to conscious reflection.

Sigmund Freud believed that the unconscious mind was a central aspect of human behavior and personality. He proposed that the unconscious mind was a repository for repressed and forgotten memories and desires, many of which were related to early childhood experiences. These repressed memories and desires were believed to exert a powerful influence on behavior and personality, often leading to the development of psychological symptoms and disorders.

Freud believed that the process of psychoanalysis could help individuals gain access to their unconscious thoughts and feelings, and thereby help them to resolve conflicts and overcome psychological symptoms. Through the use of techniques such as free association and dream analysis, psychoanalysts could help patients to uncover repressed memories and desires and integrate them into their conscious awareness.

While the concept of the unconscious mind has been criticized for its lack of empirical support, it remains an influential concept in psychology and continues to be used in psychoanalytic theory and practice. Today, many psychologists and neuroscientists believe that the mind contains both conscious and unconscious processes and that both of these processes are important for understanding human behavior and personality.

The positive aspect is that you have the ability to bring your unconscious thoughts into consciousness, and achieving this entails activating the higher brain, specifically the prefrontal cortex. The prefrontal cortex plays a crucial role in displaying skills such as understanding others' viewpoints, addressing their needs and emotions, prioritizing empathy over judgments, bias, or stereotypes, and fostering curiosity and a willingness to learn. It is within this region that we actively listen beyond our existing knowledge, forging connections with individuals outside our comfort zones, deliberately overriding outdated behavioral patterns, and cultivating new behavioral habits. This allows us to maintain focus and an open mindset even when faced with pressure and stress.

Biases are a common part of human nature. It's important to recognize that people who exhibit biased behaviors aren't necessarily intentionally excluding others or acting maliciously. Research shows that biases often operate at an unconscious level, influencing our interactions and contributing to societal inequalities. To combat harmful biased behavior, it's essential to begin by gaining a clear understanding of what biases entail.

In general, a bias is a preference or inclination towards a particular perspective, idea, or group. In the context of data analysis and artificial intelligence (AI), bias refers to systematic errors or distortions in the collection, analysis, interpretation, or presentation of data that can result in unfair or inaccurate outcomes.

For example, a bias can occur in a dataset if certain groups or individuals are underrepresented or overrepresented, leading to inaccurate or unfair conclusions. Bias can also occur in the algorithms used to analyze data, leading to discriminatory or unfair decisions.

It is important to identify and address bias in data analysis and AI in order to ensure that outcomes are fair, accurate, and unbiased. This can be achieved through careful data collection, analysis, and interpretation, as well as by designing algorithms that are transparent, explainable, and regularly audited for bias.

Components of Bias—The ABCs

There are three components of a bias that are often referred to as the ABCs of bias.

A. Affective Component: This bias is what we would refer to as prejudice or negative feelings toward a person that is based on his or her group membership.

B. Behavioral Component: This bias refers to discrimination or the actual actions taken against a person based on their group membership.

C. Cognitive Component: This bias refers to stereotypes or generalizations about a group.

Biases frequently guide us in unforeseen and unintended directions, occasionally even leading to disagreements with our own inclinations. When individuals let these biases influence their actions towards specific groups, they can become detrimental. The most significant harm stemming from biases occurs when individuals in positions of authority act upon them.

Numerous experiments indicate that individuals who assess others with bias may overlook the opportunity to recruit exceptionally talented employees or fully recognize the abilities of others. When resistance to affirmative action arises, it serves as a vivid illustration of the challenges people face in acknowledging structural inequalities. Many individuals oppose affirmative action, fearing it may disadvantage those who are not racial minorities. This reaction could be rooted in zero-sum beliefs, perceiving gains in rights and advantages for one group as inherently leading to losses for another.

The Types of Bias

There are many different types of biases—many of which are unconscious. The biases mentioned are the ones that are seen most often within organizations.

Affinity Bias is when we have a tendency to gravitate toward people similar to ourselves. That might mean hiring or promoting someone who shares the same race, gender, age, or educational background.

Attribution Bias is when you undervalue someone's accomplishments and overvalue their mistakes depending on their gender, race, nationality, or disability status.

Beauty Bias is when you judge someone based on how attractive you think they are. People who are perceived as attractive can be viewed more positively and treated more favorably.

Confirmation Bias refers to the tendency to look for or favor information that confirms beliefs you already have.

Conformity Bias is common in group settings. This type of bias occurs when the views of others influence your views or opinions.

The Halo/Horns Effect is the tendency to put someone on a pedestal or think more highly of them after learning something impressive about them, or in contrast, perceiving someone negatively after learning something unfavorable about them.

It is important to be aware of these biases in order to identify and address them within your organization.

Recognizing Bias in Your Organization

Recognizing if and when unconscious bias is present in your organization is important.

Let's examine how bias affects the workplace.

- Bias hinders the hiring process.

- Bias affects employee experiences.

- Bias wastes the potential of an employee.

- Researchers suggest that 33% of those who report workplace bias feel alienated, and 34% withhold their own ideas and solutions from the organization.

How to Mitigate Biases

Recognizing bias within an organization can be a complex task, as it can be ingrained in the culture, policies, and practices of the organization. However, there are several steps that can be taken to identify and address bias:

Self-Awareness

Fostering self-awareness holds paramount importance in mitigating bias as it empowers individuals to acknowledge their personal biases, assumptions, and stereotypes that may impact their thoughts and actions. In the absence of self-awareness, individuals may remain oblivious to the existence of their biases or the extent to which these biases influence their decision-making and behavior.

By cultivating self-awareness, individuals can take the crucial step of recognizing their own biases and proactively addressing them. This self-awareness also makes individuals more receptive to feedback and willing to confront their own assumptions and beliefs. Consequently, this process contributes to the creation of an environment that is more inclusive and equitable, where every individual feels valued and respected.

Furthermore, self-awareness facilitates a deeper understanding of and appreciation for the perspectives of others. As individuals identify their own biases, they become more empathetic and attuned to the experiences and viewpoints of individuals from diverse backgrounds.

In sum, self-awareness serves as a vital instrument in the battle against bias, as it empowers individuals to acknowledge and confront their own biases, fostering an environment that is characterized by inclusivity and equity. This ongoing journey necessitates individuals to remain open to feedback, be willing to challenge their assumptions, and remain steadfast in their commitment to promoting diversity and inclusion.

Staff Training

Staff training is helpful for opening the channels of communication.

It is important in organizations to mitigate bias for several reasons:

- **To raise awareness:** Staff training can help raise awareness among employees about the various forms of bias that exist in society and how they can manifest themselves in the workplace. By increasing knowledge and understanding about different types of bias, employees can better recognize and address them.

- **To promote inclusivity:** Non-profit organizations often have a mission to promote inclusivity and diversity. Staff training can help employees understand how their biases can affect their interactions with others, and how they can work to create a more inclusive environment for everyone.

- **To improve decision-making:** Bias can impact decision-making, leading to unfair or discriminatory practices. By providing staff with training on how to recognize and mitigate bias, non-profit organizations can improve the quality of their decision-making processes.

- **To foster accountability:** Non-profit organizations have a responsibility to ensure that their policies and practices are fair and equitable. Staff training can help to establish a culture of accountability, where employees are encouraged to identify and address bias in their own behavior and in the organization's policies and practices.

Engaging in open dialogues about implicit bias can diminish the influence of biased behaviors among members of an organization or community. Effective training programs play a crucial role in fostering employees' awareness of the existence of unconscious bias, empowering them to proactively mitigate its impact on their decision-making and interactions in the workplace.

Research by the Equality and Human Rights Commission has underscored the significance of training in heightening awareness of unconscious bias. Participants in such training gain insights into the fact that, even when they do not consciously endorse specific labels or stereotypes, these can still subtly influence their attitudes and behaviors beyond their conscious awareness.

Revising Institutional Policies and Procedures

Revising instructional policies holds significant importance in reducing bias, as these policies can wield considerable influence over the experiences of employees. Biased policies have the potential to reinforce stereotypes, restrict opportunities, and erect obstacles to success for specific groups of employees.

Revising instructional policies can help to identify and address bias in several ways:

- **Identify and address implicit biases:** Policies can reflect the biases and assumptions of the individuals who create them. By revising policies, educators can identify and address implicit biases that may be present.

- **Promote cultural responsiveness:** Revising policies can help to promote cultural responsiveness by ensuring that policies are respectful of diverse cultures, backgrounds, and experiences.

- **Provide equitable opportunities:** Policies can serve as a means to offer equitable opportunities to every employee. Through policy revisions, organizations can establish that all employees have access to the necessary resources and support essential for their success

- **Foster an inclusive environment:** Revising policies can help to foster an inclusive environment where all employees feel valued and respected. Policies that promote diversity and inclusion can help to create a sense of belonging for employees from diverse backgrounds.

- **Ensure compliance with anti-discrimination laws:** Revising policies can help to ensure compliance with anti-discrimination laws and regulations. Policies that are discriminatory or biased can lead to legal challenges and negative publicity for organizations.

In summary, the process of revising instructional policies constitutes a critical measure in addressing bias within the workforce. Numerous institutional policies were originally crafted in a context vastly different from today's workforce. Even minor adjustments to policies can yield significant impacts on employees. Evaluating practices and policies while considering biases can pinpoint those that might place certain community members at a disadvantage. By formulating inclusive and equitable policies, organizations can contribute to ensuring that all employees are afforded equal opportunities for success.

Case Study

The Resume Study

One notable case study for implicit bias is the "Resume Study" conducted by researchers at the National Bureau of Economic Research.

In this study, researchers created identical resumes for job applicants but randomly assigned either a "white-sounding" name (such as Emily or Greg) or a "Black-sounding" name (such as Lakisha or Jamal) to each resume. They then sent the resumes to a sample of employers who had posted job openings in major American cities.

The study found that resumes with "white-sounding" names received 50% more callbacks than those with "Black-sounding" names, despite the fact that the resumes were otherwise identical. This suggests that implicit bias, or unconscious attitudes and beliefs, may be influencing hiring decisions.

The study also found that the effect of implicit bias varied depending on the job market. In fields where there were relatively few Black applicants, the effect of implicit bias was more pronounced. This suggests that implicit bias may be more likely to emerge in environments where there is less diversity.

The "Resume Study" is a powerful example of how implicit bias can shape our perceptions and behaviors, often without us even realizing it. It highlights the importance of recognizing and addressing our biases, both as individuals and as a society, in order to promote greater equality and fairness in the workplace and beyond.

Integrative Exercises

Bias Audit

One integrative exercise that organizations can do to address bias in the workplace is a Bias Audit. A bias audit involves a comprehensive review of an organization's policies, procedures, and practices to identify areas where bias may be present. The audit can be conducted by an external consultant or by a team of employees within the organization who are trained to recognize and mitigate bias.

Step 1: Define the scope of the audit

Determine the areas of the organization that will be audited, such as recruitment, hiring, performance evaluations, promotion, and compensation.

Step 2: Develop a checklist of potential biases

Create a checklist of potential biases that may be present in the organization's policies, procedures, and practices. This may include biases related to race, gender, age, sexual orientation, disability, and other factors.

Step 3: Collect data

Collect data on the organization's policies, procedures, and practices in the areas identified in step 1. This may involve reviewing documents, conducting interviews with employees, and observing work processes.

Step 4: Analyze the data

Analyze the data collected to identify areas where bias may be present. This may involve identifying patterns, trends, and discrepancies in the data.

Step 5: Develop recommendations

Based on the analysis, develop recommendations for addressing any bias identified in the organization's policies, procedures, and practices. These recommendations should be specific, actionable, and tailored to the organization's needs.

Step 6: Implement changes

Implement the recommendations developed in step 5 and monitor the effectiveness of the changes over time.

By conducting a Bias Audit, organizations can identify and address areas of bias in their policies, procedures, and practices, promoting a more inclusive and equitable workplace culture.

Chapter Seven

The Impact of Microaggressions in the Workplace

Microaggressions refer to the subtle, often unintentional, verbal, and nonverbal slights, insults, and invalidations that negatively impact marginalized individuals or groups. These seemingly small actions can accumulate over time, causing significant psychological and emotional harm to those who experience them.

The concept of microaggressions was first introduced by psychiatrist and Harvard professor Chester Pierce in the 1970s. Since then, research has shown the pervasive impact of microaggressions and their contribution to systemic inequalities.

Microaggressions can be described as death by 1,000 cuts. If someone gets a little paper cut, it's annoying. It hurts, but you are easily able to move past it. If you imagine a person who gets paper cuts constantly, it can be painful and unbearable. That is the potential harm that can impact the recipient of microaggressions.

This chapter will explore the concept of microaggressions, their impact, and ways to combat them.

Micro Messages

Micro messages refer to the subtle, often unconscious, messages that we communicate through our words, tone of voice, body language, and other nonverbal cues. These messages can be positive or negative and can have a significant impact on our relationships and interactions with others. Micro messages can be intentional or unintentional, and they can be used to convey messages of support or undermine the confidence and abilities of others.

There are several types of micro messages including microadvantages, microinsults, microinvalidations, microinequities, microaggressions, microassaults, and microaffirmations.

Microadvantage: Microadvantages are the subtle, often unconscious, advantages that individuals or groups receive in their daily interactions. These advantages can be based on a person's race, gender, sexual orientation, socio-economic status, or other personal characteristics. While often less visible than more explicit forms of advantage, such as privilege, micro advantages can have a significant impact on an individual's opportunities and success.

There are several types of microadvantages, including:

- **Access:** Microadvantages can provide individuals with greater access to resources and opportunities, such as education or employment opportunities, that may not be available to others.

- **Perception:** Microadvantages can influence how individuals are perceived by others, such as being seen as more competent, capable, or trustworthy.

- **Treatment:** Microadvantages can result in preferential treatment, such as being given more lenient disciplinary action or being granted more flexibility in their work schedule.

Microadvantages can have a significant impact on an individual's opportunities and success, particularly when they occur over time and accumulate. They can contribute to the perpetuation of systemic inequalities by providing certain individuals or groups with an unfair advantage over others. Microadvantages can also lead to a false sense of meritocracy, where individuals attribute their success solely to their own abilities and fail to recognize the role of privilege and opportunity in their achievements.

There are several ways to address microadvantages, including:

- **Awareness:** Increasing awareness of microadvantages and their impact can help individuals and organizations recognize when they are occurring and take steps to address them.

- **Equity:** Prioritizing equity in all aspects of life, such as in education, employment, and healthcare, can help create a more level playing field for individuals from all backgrounds.

- **Diversity and Inclusion:** Fostering diversity and inclusion in all aspects of life can help ensure that individuals from all backgrounds have equal access to opportunities and success.

- **Accountability:** Holding individuals and organizations accountable for their actions and decisions can help ensure that microadvantages are not perpetuated.

Microadvantages are subtle forms of advantage that can have a significant impact on an individual's opportunities and success. Understanding the impact of microadvantages and ways to address them is essential in creating a more just and equitable society. By increasing awareness, prioritizing equity, fostering diversity and inclusion, and holding individuals and organizations accountable, we can work towards a more level playing field for individuals from all backgrounds.

Microinsult: Microinsults are a form of subtle, often unintentional, communication that conveys negative messages about a person's identity, background, or characteristics. They are typically implicit or indirect and may be conveyed through nonverbal cues, tone of voice, or seemingly innocuous comments.

Examples of microinsults include comments that undermine a person's intelligence, abilities, or qualifications based on their gender, race, ethnicity, religion, or other personal characteristics. For instance, assuming that a woman is less competent than a man in a particular field or suggesting that a person of color only got a job due to affirmative action would be examples of microinsults.

Microinsults can be particularly insidious because they are often subtle enough to be dismissed or ignored, yet they can still have a damaging impact on the person receiving them. Over time, repeated microinsults can erode a person's confidence and self-esteem and contribute to a hostile or unwelcoming work or social environment.

To combat microinsults, it is important to be aware of their existence and the harm they can cause. Educating oneself and others about the subtle ways in which discrimination can manifest is a good starting point. Additionally, actively challenging microinsults when they occur, whether directed at oneself or others, can help to create a more inclusive and respectful community.

Microinvalidation: Microinvalidations are similar to microinsults in that they are also a form of subtle, often unintentional communication, that conveys negative messages about a person's identity, background, or characteristics. However, microinvalidations are different from microinsults in that they involve denying or dismissing a person's experiences or feelings related to discrimination or marginalization.

Examples of microinvalidations include statements like "I don't see color," which can minimize the experiences of people of color who face discrimination based on their race, or saying "I don't think of you as disabled," which can invalidate the experiences of people with disabilities who face barriers and discrimination based on their disability.

Microinvalidations can be harmful because they can make people feel invisible or unheard and can contribute to a sense of isolation and marginalization. This can be especially damaging in contexts where people are already facing systemic discrimination or marginalization.

To combat microinvalidations, it is important to listen to and validate people's experiences and feelings related to discrimination or marginalization. This means acknowledging that discrimination exists and that people's experiences of it are valid and real. It also means avoiding language or behaviors that deny or dismiss people's experiences or feelings. Instead, it is important to create spaces where people feel seen, heard, and valued and where their experiences and perspectives are respected and validated.

Microinequity: Microinequity refers to subtle and often unintentional behaviors or practices that result in the unequal treatment of individuals based on their identity, background, or characteristics. They are small actions or behaviors that may seem insignificant but, over time, can create a culture of exclusion and marginalization.

Examples of microinequities include things like interrupting a colleague or classmate more frequently during meetings or discussions because of their gender, race, or ethnicity; overlooking the contributions of individuals with disabilities or mental health conditions, or assuming that someone is not interested in a certain subject or activity based on their sexual orientation or gender identity.

Microinequities can be harmful because they can make individuals feel undervalued, excluded, or invisible. They can also lead to a sense of isolation and can negatively impact productivity, well-being, and job satisfaction.

To combat microinequities, it is important to recognize and understand how they can manifest in different situations. Education and training can help to raise awareness and promote understanding of how microinequities can impact individuals and teams. Creating an inclusive culture that values diversity and encourages open communication can also help to reduce microinequities. Additionally, providing opportunities for individuals to give feedback and share their experiences can help to identify and address microinequities in the workplace or other settings.

Microaggression: Microaggressions are subtle, often unintentional, verbal or nonverbal behaviors or actions that communicate negative or derogatory messages towards people based on their identity, background, or characteristics. They can be experienced by individuals from marginalized groups and are often rooted in stereotypes or prejudices.

Examples of microaggressions include things like asking a person of color where they are "really" from, suggesting that a woman is not qualified for a job because of her gender, or assuming that someone with a disability needs help without asking first.

Microaggressions can be harmful because they can make individuals feel invalidated, disrespected, and excluded. They can also contribute to a hostile or unwelcoming environment and can negatively impact mental health and well-being.

To combat microaggressions, it is important to recognize and understand how they can manifest in different situations. Education and training can help to raise awareness and promote understanding of how microaggressions can impact individuals and teams. It is also important to create a culture that values diversity and encourages open communication, where individuals feel safe to speak up and challenge microaggressions when they occur. Additionally, fostering a sense of empathy and understanding towards others can help to reduce microaggressions and promote a more inclusive and respectful environment.

Microassault: Microassaults are explicit and intentional verbal or nonverbal behaviors or actions that communicate derogatory or discriminatory messages towards people based on their identity, background, or characteristics. They can be experienced by individuals from marginalized groups and are often overt forms of discrimination.

Examples of microassaults include things like using racial slurs or derogatory language towards an individual, making sexist or homophobic jokes, or displaying symbols of hate or intolerance.

Microassaults can be extremely harmful and can cause significant emotional and psychological distress to the individuals targeted. They can also create a hostile or unsafe environment and can contribute to a culture of discrimination and intolerance.

To combat microassaults, it is important to have clear policies and procedures in place to address and prevent discriminatory behavior. Education and training can also help to raise awareness and promote understanding of the impact of microassaults on individuals and communities. It is important to hold individuals accountable for their behavior and to create a safe and inclusive environment where everyone is valued and respected. Additionally, providing support and resources for those who have experienced microassaults can help to promote healing and resilience.

Microaffirmations: Microaffirmations are small, subtle, and often unconscious positive gestures or behaviors that people use to support, validate, and show respect for others. These small acts can include things like using someone's name when addressing them, making eye contact, nodding in agreement, or offering words of encouragement.

Microaffirmations can be especially important for people who belong to historically marginalized or underrepresented groups, as they can help counteract the negative effects of implicit bias and discrimination. By providing small but meaningful acts of recognition and validation, microaffirmations can help create a more inclusive and supportive environment for everyone.

The concept of microaffirmations was first introduced by Mary Rowe, an MIT administrator and scholar, in the early 2000s. Since then, it has gained recognition in fields like psychology, sociology, and organizational behavior as a way to promote diversity, equity, and inclusion in various settings, including workplaces, schools, and communities.

While microaffirmations may seem small and insignificant, they can have a powerful impact on people's sense of belonging, confidence, and well-being. By creating a culture of respect and support, we can help build more inclusive communities and workplaces where everyone feels valued and empowered.

How are Microaggressions Like Mosquito Bites?

Fusion Comedy has produced a video on microaggressions. They present microaggressions as mosquito bites. Getting bit once by a mosquito won't harm you, but if you get bit enough times, then there is a higher risk of developing West Nile virus, yellow fever, or malaria; this is the same for microaggressions. They seem harmless, like mosquito bites but can have long-lasting harmful effects. There is clearly a cumulative impact of microaggressions that can be traumatic and painful for the recipient.

View this video on YouTube here:
https://www.youtube.com/watch?v=nQ9l7y4UuxY

Your Response to the Awareness of Your Microaggressions

How do you respond when someone points out that you are engaged in microaggression? What do you do when you have become aware of your own microaggressive comments or attitudes?

Initially, your response might be to defend your intention and displace the blame. For example, you might find yourself saying, "Well, you completely misunderstood what I was saying. I was just joking. Why are you being so sensitive?"

In order to be successful in addressing a microaggression, you want to focus on the impact of the microaggression. Be willing to listen with the intention of understanding what happened and how you may have contributed to causing pain.

Micro interventions address microaggressions. In the next section, we'll discuss how to know when you need to address an issue of microaggression in the workplace.

Addressing Micro Intervention in Three Steps

Micro interventions are strategies to address and respond to microaggressions, which are subtle, often unintentional acts or comments that perpetuate stereotypes and marginalize individuals based on their race, gender, ethnicity, or other social identities. These interventions aim to create a more inclusive and respectful environment.

Here are three steps to perform a micro intervention:

Step 1: Assess the Situation

- Before intervening, take a moment to assess the situation. Ask yourself if it's safe to intervene and if you feel comfortable doing so.

- Determine whether what you witnessed or experienced qualifies as a microaggression. Microaggressions can be subtle, so it's essential to recognize them.

- Consider your relationship with the person involved and the dynamics of the situation. Are you better positioned to address the issue, or would it be more effective if someone else stepped in?

Step 2: Choose Your Approach

There are different ways to address microaggressions, and the approach you choose should be tailored to the specific situation and your comfort level.

Here are some approaches to consider:

- **Direct Confrontation:** If you feel safe and comfortable, you can address the microaggression directly by calmly and assertively pointing out the problematic behavior. For example, you might say, "I don't think that comment is appropriate because it perpetuates a stereotype."

- **Ask Clarifying Questions:** If you're unsure whether the behavior was intentional, you can ask clarifying questions to encourage reflection. For example, "Can you explain what you meant by that?"

- **Support the Target:** If you're not comfortable confronting the perpetrator directly, you can provide support to the person targeted by the microaggression. Offer words of encouragement or empathy and let them know you're there for them.

- **Use Humor or Sarcasm:** In some situations, using humor or sarcasm can help disarm the microaggressor without escalating the conflict. However, be cautious with this approach, as it may not always be effective and can backfire.

- **Educate Privately:** If you have a close relationship with the person responsible for the microaggression, you can choose to educate them privately about the impact of their words or actions.

Step 3: Follow Up and Offer Resources

- After addressing the microaggression, it's essential to follow up and ensure that the issue is resolved or that the person understands the impact of their behavior.

- Offer resources for further education on diversity, equity, and inclusion, such as books, articles, workshops, or training programs.

- Continue to be an ally and advocate for a more inclusive environment, not only in that specific instance but also in your ongoing interactions and conversations.

Remember that micro interventions are most effective when done with empathy, respect, and a genuine desire to promote understanding and change. The goal is to create a culture where microaggressions are recognized and discouraged, leading to a more inclusive and respectful community or workplace.

Case Study

Dr. Yaba Blay and Black Identity

One case study about microaggressions involves a Black female university professor named Dr. Yaba Blay. Dr. Blay teaches Africana Studies at Drexel University and also conducts research on Black identity and representation.

In 2014, Dr. Blay participated in a live television interview on a popular morning news program to discuss her work and her recently published book. During the interview, the interviewer repeatedly referred to Dr. Blay as "African American" even though she had previously stated that she identifies as Black. Dr. Blay attempted to correct the interviewer by saying, "I identify as Black," but the interviewer continued to use the term "African American" throughout the interview.

This incident is an example of microaggression, which is a subtle or indirect form of discrimination or prejudice that is often unintentional but can still have harmful effects. In this case, the interviewer's repeated use of the term "African American" undermined Dr. Blay's personal identity and agency by imposing a label that she did not identify with.

Dr. Blay later wrote about the incident on her blog and used it as an opportunity to educate people about the importance of respecting individuals' self-identified racial and ethnic identities. She explained that while the term "African American" may be a common way to refer to Black people in the United States, it is not always accurate or appropriate and may not reflect how individuals actually identify themselves.

This case study underscores the importance of recognizing and addressing microaggressions in our society.

Integrative Exercise

Impact of Microaggressions

Have you heard/seen these or personally thought about them?

Each group should dialogue about the statement that corresponds to your group number. Group 1 will discuss statement #1, group 2 discuss statement #2, and so on. Take some time to reflect on your own experiences with micro messages. Think about a time when you may have experienced or witnessed a micro message and how it made you feel.

- Have you had one of these statements directed towards you or have you directed the statement towards another person?

- How might these actions or statements be hurtful or invalidating?

- Brainstorm strategies for addressing and preventing micro messages.

Statement, Action, or Thought	I have observed	I personally said/thought
Microadvantage		
1. Assumption of the same access to resources (privilege) - *"If I can do this, so can you."*		
Microinvalidation		
2. *"I don't see color," "I don't think of you as disabled."*		
Microinsult		
3. Assuming that a woman is less competent than a man in a particular field or suggesting that a person of color only got a job due to affirmative action.		
Micro inequity		
4. Interrupting a colleague or classmate more frequently during meetings or discussions because of their gender, race, or ethnicity; overlooking the contributions of individuals with disabilities or mental health conditions; or assuming that someone is not interested in a certain subject or activity based on their sexual orientation or gender identity.		
Micro assault		
5. Using racial slurs or derogatory language toward an individual, making sexist or homophobic jokes, or displaying symbols of hate or intolerance.		
Microaggression		
6. Asking a person of color where they are *"really"* from, suggesting that a woman is not qualified for a job because of her gender, or assuming that someone with a disability needs help without asking first.		

Chapter Eight

Managing Power & Privilege in Leadership

I n this chapter, we will discuss how managing power and privilege in leadership is beneficial to an organization. Leadership is a complex and nuanced concept that can be defined in many ways. While there are various models of leadership, most of them emphasize the importance of power and privilege in leading others. Power and privilege are two concepts that are often intertwined and can be used as both tools and obstacles in leadership. In this chapter, we will explore how leaders can manage their power and privilege in order to create a more inclusive and equitable workplace.

Let's first clarify their definitions.

Privilege refers to the right or exemption from liability or duty that's granted as a special benefit or advantage.

Power, in this context, refers to the capacity to exercise control over others by deciding what's best for them. It encompasses deciding who will have access to or denial from resources.

The following terms are used to define social groups that society has afforded more or less power.

Marginalized/Oppressed/Disadvantaged are the social groups with less power, less access, and less privilege. They are considered social groups that have been disenfranchised, invisible, dehumanized, and exploited.

Dominant/Privileged/Advantaged are social groups who have the ability to navigate the world without consequences due to unearned advantages at the expense of folks who are marginalized.

Power is the ability to influence others and make decisions that affect their lives. It can be derived from a variety of sources, such as one's position in an organization, their expertise, or their ability to control resources. Privilege, on the other hand, is the unearned advantages that people have based on their social identity characteristics such as race, gender, sexual orientation, or socioeconomic status. Privilege can manifest in many ways, such as easier access to opportunities, greater authority in decision-making, or more positive assumptions about one's abilities.

Privilege

Privilege is a concept that has gained increased attention in recent years, particularly in discussions of social justice and equity. Privilege is interconnected with power in our society. Those who have privilege have the ability to create and maintain societal norms, often to their benefit and at the expense of others. Privilege does not mean that a person has not experienced struggles or that their life has not been difficult. Being privileged does not mean that you did not work hard for the things that you have. Privilege is fluid. It can change as you move through life. It's also contextual. Identities you hold can give you an advantage, whereas they can give another person a disadvantage based on how people perceive you.

Privilege is often invisible to those who have it, but its effects are visible in society. Privilege can manifest in many ways, such as easier access to education, job opportunities, healthcare, and political power. Privilege can also include more subtle advantages, such as not being subjected to stereotyping, microaggressions, or discrimination based on one's social identity characteristics.

Privilege has strategically been set up as a taboo subject, allowing those who are in dominant groups to ignore and embed often invisible forms of oppression. When we refer to someone having privilege, what we want you to consider is their accessibility and access to resources. Those in power generally have unearned access to things that empower them, and typically members of marginalized groups do not have access to them.

This notion of unearned access is where the inequity lies because access is based on an identity someone holds that has traditionally been associated with power. To put this into perspective, let's look at white privilege.

People who are white have access to resources that work in their favor as opposed to people of color who experience a multitude of barriers to gaining access to the same resources. These barriers are rooted in historical inequities. They include systems, policies and laws that disenfranchise people of color. White people are not forced to question their behaviors because the system is set up to afford them that luxury.

A good example is a white child is often not taught how to interact with authority figures like the police, whereas, for significant safety reasons, a child of color is taught this lesson. If you do not have to think about it, most often, it is because you have privilege.

Privilege operates on both individual and systemic levels. On an individual level, privilege can affect how people perceive themselves and others and how they interact with others. On a systemic level, privilege can shape the structures and institutions of society and create inequalities that persist over time.

Types of Privilege

There are many different types of privilege, including:

- **White Privilege:** The advantages and benefits that white people receive in society due to their race.

- **Male Privilege:** The advantages and benefits that men receive in society due to their gender.

- **Heterosexual Privilege:** The advantages and benefits that heterosexual people receive in society due to their sexual orientation.

- **Cisgender Privilege:** The advantages and benefits that individuals who identify with the gender they were assigned at birth receive in society.

- **Able-bodied Privilege:** The advantages and benefits that individuals who do not have disabilities receive in society.

- **Socioeconomic Privilege:** The advantages and benefits that individuals from higher income or wealth backgrounds receive in society.

Privilege can have both positive and negative impacts on individuals and society. On an individual level, privilege can lead to feelings of entitlement, superiority, and disconnection from others who do not share the same privileges. It can also lead to a lack of understanding or awareness of the experiences and realities of those who do not have the same privileges.

On a societal level, privilege can perpetuate inequalities and create barriers to social mobility and opportunity. Privilege can also lead to the marginalization and oppression of individuals and groups who do not have the same privileges and can result in systemic discrimination and exclusion.

Addressing and Dismantling Privilege

Addressing and dismantling privilege requires a multi-faceted approach that involves both individual and systemic change. To address privilege, it is important to acknowledge and understand it and to recognize how it operates in our own lives and in society at large. This requires self-reflection and a willingness to listen to the experiences of others who do not share our privileges. It also requires a commitment to taking action to challenge and change the systems and structures that perpetuate privilege and inequality.

One way to address privilege is through education and awareness-raising. This can involve learning about the experiences of marginalized groups, examining the ways in which privilege operates in different areas of society, and challenging our own assumptions and biases. It can also involve engaging in conversations with others about privilege and inequality and working to create spaces where people can share their experiences and perspectives in a safe and respectful manner.

Another way to address privilege is through activism and advocacy. This can involve supporting policies and initiatives that aim to promote equity and justice, such as affirmative action programs or campaigns for living wages and affordable housing. It can also involve working to dismantle systems and structures that perpetuate privilege and inequality, such as challenging discriminatory hiring practices or advocating for the reform of the criminal justice system.

Dismantling Privilege

Dismantling privilege is a more radical and transformative approach that seeks to fundamentally change the systems and structures perpetuating inequality. This requires a deep understanding of the ways in which privilege operates and a commitment to challenging and changing those systems at a systemic level.

Dismantling privilege involves challenging the power structures and institutions perpetuating privilege and inequality. This can involve advocating for radical social and economic reforms, such as the redistribution of wealth and resources, or the creation of new systems and structures that prioritize equity and justice. It can also involve working to dismantle oppressive systems, such as white supremacy or heteronormativity, and advocating for the rights and dignity of marginalized communities.

Dismantling privilege requires a sustained and collective effort, as it involves challenging deeply entrenched power structures and narratives that have existed for centuries. However, it is also a necessary and urgent task, as the perpetuation of privilege and inequality has devastating consequences for individuals and communities who are marginalized and oppressed.

Intersectionality and Privilege

It is important to recognize that privilege operates in **intersectional** ways, meaning that individuals can have multiple social identities that intersect to create unique experiences of privilege and oppression. For example, a white woman may experience privilege based on her race but may also experience oppression based on her gender. Similarly, a wealthy person with a disability may experience privilege based on their socioeconomic status but may also face barriers and discrimination based on their disability.

Recognizing and addressing **intersectionality** is therefore crucial in addressing and dismantling privilege. This involves understanding how systems and structures of privilege and oppression intersect and interact with each other and working to create solutions that address the complex and overlapping forms of inequality that people experience.

Addressing and dismantling privilege is a complex and ongoing process that requires a deep understanding of the ways in which privilege operates in society, as well as a commitment to challenging and changing the systems and structures that perpetuate inequality. This involves self-reflection, education, activism, and collective action, as well as recognizing the intersectional ways in which privilege and oppression operate. By working together to address and dismantle privilege, we can create a more just and equitable society for all.

Power Dynamics at Work

Despite organizational charts and management policies, most individuals don't really understand what gives us power and the different ways that we can use that power in the workplace. Let's break down some of these types of powers to better understand what dynamic exists within a team and how your organization can build power in more intentional and equitable ways.

It's important to increase the capacity of executive leaders at middle and senior levels by providing information on the dynamics of power in healthy organizations. This is an important topic because understanding power and learning how to use it are critical skills for leaders. It's essential to the overall health and sustainability of an organization.

Two critical elements that are involved in understanding and using power center around the concepts of shared power and empowerment, both of which occur in the context of the relationship between leaders and followers and the health of these relationships throughout the entire organization. In healthy organizations, the use of power is balanced, and it is shared. It's used in ways that encourage and empower others to act for the strength of the organization. In order to be an effective leader, you must be able to use the power within your organization to produce results.

Organizations that understand the connection between leadership and power and how to use both effectively will have a healthier, more productive, and more sustainable organization.

Power Dynamics

Power is the ability to influence others and achieve desired outcomes. There are two ways that we use power. There is **power over** and **power with**.

Power over usually occurs in the workplace when it's used to control another person or group. Those who have the most power can set standards, policies, and processes for others to comply with.

Power with provides space and empowers others to offer their perspectives, insights, and their experiences. It demands the dismantling of traditional hierarchies, and it works collaboratively by leveraging the talents and skills of the group. You might not realize it, but the power dynamics inside an office, inside a business, can slowly destroy the organization's culture by breeding an environment of fear and mistrust and ultimately stemming from a desire to control others.

Power dynamics often manifest themselves through the misuse of privilege in relation to those who are often marginalized or underrepresented in the workplace or society. We see examples in play where people in positions of power or influence, who also hold privileged characteristics, promote and propagate a workplace environment where racism, sexism, ableism, or homophobic views and beliefs are allowed to take place. They are allowed to take hold and grow.

In turn, it destroys a company's culture. Where organizations do not actively address power and privilege dynamics born out of nepotism, bullying, harassment, or exclusion, this will ultimately breed and cause toxicity to fester, which will, in turn, destroy the psychological safety that the staff and colleagues are entitled to feel.

When this happens, a working environment will experience a decline in morale and motivation, an increase in absenteeism and staff turnover, a deterioration in customer service and quality, and a drop in productivity levels which often leads to a loss of revenue.

Creating a Healthy Workplace

In today's fast-paced and interconnected world, creating a healthy workplace environment is vital for the success and well-being of both employees and organizations. As a leader, it is your responsibility to actively seek out and address toxic power dynamics that may be undermining your company's culture. In order to improve your culture and create a healthy workplace environment, it's essential as a leader you take those steps to actively seek out and break down those toxic power dynamics.

In organizations, power can be categorized into various types, including:

- **Legitimate Power:** This power is derived from a leader's formal position within the organization. It is the authority granted to individuals based on their job titles and responsibilities.

- **Reward Power:** This type of power stems from a leader's ability to provide rewards, such as salary increases, promotions, or recognition, to employees who comply with their directives.

- **Coercive Power:** Coercive power relies on the ability to apply punishments or negative consequences to those who do not comply with the leader's wishes.

- **Expert Power:** Leaders with expert power possess specialized knowledge, skills, or expertise that others value and respect.

- **Referent Power:** Referent power is based on the personal charisma, likability, and admiration that a leader commands from their followers.

In order to break down those power dynamics, an organization will want to ensure that they improve their culture and create a healthy workplace environment. It is essential, as a leader, that you take those steps to actively seek out and break down those toxic power dynamics. You will want to encourage open communication and create an environment where employees feel comfortable speaking up about their concerns and sharing their opinions, even if they differ from those of their superiors.

This also means giving employees the opportunity to share their ideas and suggestions for how things can be improved.

Another way to break down power dynamics in the workplace is to encourage collaboration. This means creating opportunities for employees to work together on projects and tasks. When employees are encouraged to collaborate, they're more likely to feel they are part of a team instead of feeling like they are pitted against each other.

This will help you establish a culture of humility and vulnerability by ensuring that people are allowed to grow, learn, and develop without fear of recrimination for making mistakes. Everyone should feel that they are in a supportive environment where their colleagues have their back, and their supervisor or manager is there to help them.

You will want to create clear information and process channels. By having clearly defined channels through which information flows between managers and their teams. This also means ensuring that these channels are open and accessible to all employees, where employees are less likely to feel like they are being left out or excluded from important decision-making processes.

Lastly, as leaders, you will want to promote diversity, equity, inclusion, and belonging. Ensure that everyone feels like they belong by valuing different perspectives and experiences. This includes things like implementing flexible working arrangements and offering unconscious bias training.

Case Study

Transforming a Toxic Workplace Culture

In this case study, we explore the journey of a mid-sized tech company, which faced significant challenges due to toxic power dynamics within its workplace culture. As the negative impact on employee morale and productivity became evident, the company's leadership decided to take proactive steps to address and dismantle these toxic patterns. This case study showcases the strategies implemented by the company to create a healthier and more inclusive work environment.

Company Background

The company, which was founded a decade ago, initially enjoyed a reputation as an innovative and employee-centric organization. However, as the company grew and underwent leadership changes, subtle power struggles started to emerge. Over time, these struggles evolved into toxic power dynamics, leading to a sharp decline in employee satisfaction, high turnover rates, and decreased productivity.

Identifying the Problem

The signs of toxic power dynamics were evident in various ways. Middle managers excessively controlled their teams, stifling creativity and reducing employee autonomy. Fear-based leadership was observed, with employees reluctant to voice concerns or provide feedback for fear of retribution. This led to a culture of silence, where issues were left unresolved, and conflicts simmered beneath the surface.

The company's once-strong team spirit had disintegrated as favoritism became apparent in the distribution of rewards and opportunities. Furthermore, the lack of transparency in decision-making led to a pervasive sense of distrust among employees, who felt disconnected from the organization's direction.

Intervention Strategies

Recognizing the urgency to address these challenges and rebuild a healthy workplace culture, the company launched a comprehensive intervention plan, which included:

Cultural Assessment: The company engaged external consultants to conduct a thorough cultural assessment. This involved surveys, interviews, and focus groups with employees at all levels to gauge their perceptions of the existing culture and identify areas of concern.

Leadership Development: The company recognized the need to invest in developing its leaders. Senior executives and middle managers participated in intensive workshops on emotional intelligence, effective communication, and leadership coaching—the training aimed to improve self-awareness and cultivate a more empathetic and inclusive leadership style.

Employee Feedback Initiatives: To encourage open communication and break the culture of silence, the company established regular feedback sessions. A confidential online platform allowed employees to submit suggestions, concerns, and ideas anonymously. Management committed to addressing these submissions and providing transparent updates on the actions taken.

Diversity and Inclusion Initiatives: To combat favoritism and create a more equitable environment, the company implemented diversity and inclusion initiatives. This included updating hiring practices to ensure a diverse talent pool, forming employee resource groups, and launching mentorship programs.

Team Building and Collaboration Activities: The company organized team-building events and cross-functional collaboration projects to foster a sense of unity and cooperation. These initiatives helped bridge gaps between teams and reduced silos.

Results

Over time, the company experienced significant positive changes as a result of its intervention strategies:

Increased Employee Satisfaction: The cultural assessment conducted six months after the intervention revealed a notable increase in employee satisfaction levels. Employees reported feeling more valued, heard, and supported.

Reduced Turnover: The company saw a decline in employee turnover rates as the workplace culture became more positive and inclusive. Talented individuals were more likely to stay with the organization, reducing recruitment and training costs.

Enhanced Productivity: With a more collaborative and empowering work environment, employees demonstrated higher levels of motivation and productivity.

Improved Innovation and Creativity: As employees felt more comfortable sharing ideas and taking risks, innovation and creativity flourished within the organization.

This company's case study exemplifies the transformative power of addressing toxic power dynamics to create a healthier workplace culture. By investing in leadership development, encouraging open communication, promoting diversity and inclusion, and fostering collaboration, the organization was able to rebuild trust, boost employee morale, and achieve greater success. The journey towards a healthy workplace culture is ongoing, but the company's commitment to continuous improvement sets an inspiring example for other organizations to follow.

Integrative Exercise

Power Dynamics

The following exercise is designed to help organizations identify and address toxic power dynamics to create a healthy workplace culture. This exercise promotes self-awareness, open communication, and collaborative problem-solving among employees and leaders.

This exercise can be completed in a half-day workshop or broken down into multiple shorter sessions, depending on the organization's size and needs.

Materials Needed

- Whiteboard or flipchart

- Markers and sticky notes

- Handouts on different types of power in organizations and signs of toxic power dynamics

Step 1: Setting the Stage

- Start by explaining the importance of a healthy workplace culture and how toxic power dynamics can negatively impact employees and the organization as a whole.

- Provide an overview of the different types of power in organizations and the signs of toxic power dynamics using the handouts. Encourage participants to reflect on their own experiences and observations.

Step 2: Toxic Power Dynamics Brainstorming

- Divide participants into small groups and assign each group a specific type of power (legitimate, reward, coercive, expert, referent). Ask each group to brainstorm potential positive and negative scenarios related to their assigned type of power.

- Participants should consider how this power can be used in healthy ways to motivate and empower employees and how it can lead to toxic dynamics if misused or abused.

- Have each group present their scenarios and discuss them as a larger group. Encourage open and respectful dialogue.

Step 3: Identifying Toxic Power Dynamics

- Distribute sticky notes to each participant. Ask participants to individually write down any instances of toxic power dynamics they have witnessed or experienced in the workplace.

- These can be anonymous to ensure openness. Collect the sticky notes and group them into categories based on the type of toxic power dynamic.

- Display the categorized sticky notes on a whiteboard or flipchart. Discuss the patterns and common themes that emerge.

Step 4: Reflection and Self-Assessment

- Provide each participant with a self-assessment questionnaire related to their leadership style and how they use their power.

- Encourage participants to take some time to reflect on their responses privately.

Step 5: Group Sharing and Action Planning

- Divide participants into new groups, mixing individuals from different teams and hierarchical levels to encourage diverse perspectives.

- Have participants share insights from their self-assessment and discuss any realizations about their use of power.

- Facilitate a discussion on how the organization can collectively address toxic power dynamics and build a healthier workplace culture.

- Encourage the groups to develop action plans with specific strategies and initiatives to foster positive changes. These may include training programs, mentorship opportunities, regular feedback sessions, and communication improvements.

Step 6: Closing

- Reconvene as a whole group and have each small group present their action plans.

- Summarize the key takeaways and emphasize the importance of ongoing commitment to building a healthy workplace culture.

- Discuss how the organization can implement and monitor the action plans effectively.

Conclusion

This integrative exercise empowers employees and leaders to collaboratively address toxic power dynamics and work towards building a healthy workplace culture. By promoting open communication, self-reflection, and action planning, organizations can create a positive environment where everyone feels valued and motivated to contribute their best.

Chapter Nine

Evaluating Agency Operations with an Equity Lens

As societal awareness of systemic inequalities and social injustices grows, it becomes increasingly crucial for agencies to assess their operations through an equity lens. An equity lens is a framework that helps organizations identify and address disparities and ensure fair treatment for all individuals, regardless of their background or characteristics. In this chapter, we will explore the importance of evaluating agency operations through an equity lens, the key elements of this process, and practical strategies for implementing equity-centered evaluation methods.

Understanding Equity in Agency Operations

Equity in agency operations refers to the fair and just treatment of all stakeholders, including employees, clients, partners, and the community. It involves recognizing and mitigating biases and barriers that may hinder access to resources, opportunities, and services. Evaluating agency operations with an equity lens is essential for promoting inclusivity, diversity, and social justice within the organization's framework.

The Benefits of an Equity-Centered Approach

An equity-centered approach refers to a framework and set of principles that prioritize fairness, justice, and equal opportunities for all individuals, particularly those who have historically been marginalized and disadvantaged. This approach is often applied in various contexts, including education, healthcare, business, and social policy. The benefits of adopting an equity-centered approach are numerous and can have a positive impact on individuals, communities, and society as a whole.

Here are some key benefits:

Improved Outcomes: Agencies that prioritize equity in their operations tend to achieve better outcomes and provide more effective services to their target populations.

Enhanced Community Trust: By demonstrating a commitment to fairness and inclusivity, agencies can build stronger relationships with the communities they serve, fostering trust and cooperation.

Attracting and Retaining Talent: A workplace that values equity is more attractive to diverse talent and is more likely to retain employees who feel valued and supported.

Increased Innovation: Embracing diverse perspectives and experiences encourages innovation, creativity, and problem-solving from a broader range of voices.

Key Elements of Evaluating Agency Operations with an Equity Lens

Evaluating agency operations with an equity lens is essential to ensure that government agencies, nonprofit organizations, and other entities are effectively addressing the needs of all members of society, especially those who have historically been marginalized or disadvantaged.

Here are key elements to consider when conducting such evaluations:

Data Collection and Analysis: Assessing equity requires collecting and analyzing relevant data disaggregated by demographic characteristics (e.g., race, gender, age, socio-economic status) to identify disparities and trends.

Impact Assessment: Examine the potential impacts of agency policies, practices, and decisions on different groups within the organization and its stakeholders.

Inclusive Stakeholder Engagement: Involve a diverse group of stakeholders in the evaluation process, ensuring that their voices and perspectives are heard and integrated into decision-making.

Culturally Responsive Evaluation: Use evaluation methods that consider cultural contexts and avoid perpetuating cultural biases in data collection and analysis.

Strategies for Implementing an Equity-Centered Evaluation

Implementing an equity-centered evaluation requires a deliberate and thoughtful approach.

Here are strategies to consider when incorporating equity into your evaluation process:

Establish Clear Equity Goals: Define specific and measurable equity goals that align with the agency's mission and values.

Review Policies and Procedures: Evaluate existing policies and procedures to identify potential biases and barriers that may impede equity.

Train Staff on Equity and Cultural Competency: Provide comprehensive training for staff to enhance their understanding of equity, cultural competency, and unconscious biases.

Incorporate Equity Metrics: Integrate equity metrics into performance evaluations and regularly track progress towards equity goals.

Address Root Causes: Go beyond surface-level solutions by addressing the root causes of disparities within agency operations.

Collaborate with the Community: Engage with community members and stakeholders to gain insights into the lived experiences and needs of the people being served.

Periodic Evaluation: Continuously reassess and refine the equity evaluation process to ensure its relevance and effectiveness over time.

Strategic Diversity, Equity, Inclusion, and Belonging Action Plan

A strategic diversity, equity, inclusion, and belonging action plan can help an organization make the most of its diversity by creating an inclusive, equitable, and sustainable culture and work environment.

Workplace diversity is the collective mixture of differences and similarities that include individual and organizational characteristics, values, beliefs, experiences, backgrounds, preferences, and behaviors.

Employers use diversity, equity, inclusion, and belonging initiatives for compliance obligations and to increase the overall bottom line with a more diverse, equitable, and inclusive workforce. Developing a DEIB initiative involves four main phases: 1) data collection and analysis to determine the need for a change strategy designed to match business objectives, 2) implementation of the initiative, 3) evaluation, and 4) continuing audit of the plan.

When developing a plan, the following components should be aligned to work with an organization's overall strategy. The sample questions to consider and/or the action steps to take are included for each component.

An organization needs to gather data; employers must know about what their workforce looks like compared with the labor market and if there are inequities based on demographics. By capturing data on employee demographics, an employer can better understand the diversity of its employees and the equity of its internal practices, identifying any areas of concern or trends.

Demographic data may include age, disability, ethnicity, national origin, family status, gender, gender identity or expression, generation, language, life experiences, organization, function and level, personality type, physical characteristics, sex, race, religion, belief and spirituality, sexual orientation, thinking and learning styles and veteran status.

Multiple resources are available to capture this data. Some employers may already have much of this information available in their HR system for affirmative action plans or EEO reporting obligations. However, most employers will need to survey their workforce through voluntary self-identification surveys to obtain additional data, such as religion and sexual orientation. It might be a challenge to gather diversity data from employees initially, especially when employees are unsure how the data will be used or if there is a general distrust of leadership in an organization.

If this is the case, an employer may want to use a third party with survey technology to capture information that will be reported in a group without identifying that information. In addition, it would be useful to gather information about the current company's culture regarding DEIB so that surveying employees can shed light on their perception of the organization in relation to encouraging and appreciating DEIB in the workplace.

Once the data is collected, underrepresented or problematic areas can be identified. To do this, employers should be given a high-level review of demographics such as age, sex, race representation, and equity and continue to drill down by location, department, and position. Identifying the problem areas can also include an inquiry if management is primarily older white males. Another inquiry will be whether there is diversity within management and leadership teams.

Do Black females make less than their white counterparts in the same position? Does the accounting department tend to hire only females? Have promotions been limited for those with English as their second language? The information gained from employee surveys can help identify other areas of concern.

Employee attitudes and culture may or may not match the survey results. If they do match, the employer has a clear path toward what needs to change. If not, the organization may want to conduct employee focus groups to better understand this disconnect. If the results indicate little to no diversity and sexual orientation or religion, it is possible that individuals don't have trust in the organization to divulge that personal information.

As suggested in the previous step, employers should outsource the data collection or use other means to collect data anonymously. Employers must determine if there are barriers impeding the employment, opportunity, or inclusion of individuals from different demographic groups.

Organizations should consider if any policies or practices need to be eliminated or adjusted. Some examples include bereavement leave to encompass all family members rather than just immediate family. The traditional definition of family has evolved, embracing diverse family structures and relationships. By extending bereavement support to all family members, organizations foster a culture of inclusivity and empathy, acknowledging the significance of various relationships in employees' lives. Such revisions not only demonstrate compassion during times of loss but also promote employee well-being, loyalty, and productivity, as individuals are empowered to grieve and honor their broader support networks within the workplace.

Despite advancements in diversity and inclusion efforts, hiring biases continue to plague organizations worldwide. These biases, often unconscious and unintentional, can be influenced by factors such as gender, race, age, appearance, and socioeconomic background. They hinder the recruitment of a diverse and talented workforce, depriving companies of valuable perspectives and skills. By examining the various types of hiring biases, understanding their consequences, and implementing proactive measures to counteract them, organizations can build a more inclusive and equitable hiring process that fosters innovation and success for all.

Assessing company culture to see if there are apparent preferences toward pro-life, traditional marriage, and other aspects often associated with religious beliefs that can repel candidates of different beliefs or lifestyles. Annual Christmas parties and recognizing only Christian holidays present the unintentional workplace message that only Christian employees are welcome. Employers might consider holding a holiday party instead and providing floating holidays that employees may use for many religious observances.

In today's politically polarized world, individuals may hold strong beliefs and affiliations, leading to potential tensions and divisions at work. The expression of political views may inadvertently lead to biases in hiring, promotions, and day-to-day interactions. Political preferences may be noticed in an employer's choice of political signs or messages on its property that may discourage individuals with different viewpoints from applying. A bumper sticker on an employee's car supporting a candidate who differs from a manager's choice may affect the manager's perception of the employee, as well as the manager's decisions regarding pay performance and promotion.

Organizations must be vigilant in recognizing and addressing such biases to ensure that employees feel respected and included, regardless of their political leanings. By fostering open dialogue, promoting empathy, and setting clear guidelines for respectful discourse, workplaces can become spaces that embrace diverse perspectives, allowing for constructive discussions and the cultivation of a more harmonious and collaborative work environment. Identifying how a diverse, equitable, and inclusive workforce can aid in achieving objectives aligned with the organization's strategy is the next step in the process.

The organization has to set specific goals related to DEIB based on the organization's strategic objectives. While DEIB initiatives have gained momentum across industries, true transformation requires a deliberate alignment with the broader vision and mission of the organization. By setting specific DEIB goals that are intertwined with strategic objectives, organizations can foster a more inclusive culture, leverage diverse perspectives, and drive sustainable growth and success. For example, an organization might have an objective to transform its teams. They might say they want to build teams that empower a collaborative culture that promotes information sharing, DEIB, and a competent and high-performing workforce to best serve their clients and their community, and the families they serve.

As its clients become more diverse, the organization is responding by embracing a more diverse and inclusive workforce to better serve its population.

For a DEIB initiative to succeed, there has to be senior-level buy-in and support. When top leadership understands the business case for DEIB and recognizes its direct links to the organization's strategic goals, they are more likely to prioritize and invest in these initiatives. Senior leaders play a significant role in driving cultural change and setting the tone for inclusivity throughout the organization.

Identifying a senior-level champion is also essential in sustaining the momentum of DEIB initiatives. This champion serves as a visible role model, advocating for DEIB at all levels of the organization and ensuring that the initiative remains a priority over time. This person is responsible for engaging and inspiring others, fostering a supportive and inclusive environment, and holding all stakeholders accountable for their commitment to DEIB.

Ultimately, when senior management actively supports DEIB initiatives and demonstrates their commitment through actions, it sends a powerful message to the entire organization. This encouragement not only fosters a diverse and inclusive workplace but also drives innovation, boosts employee morale, and positively impacts the organization's overall performance and bottom line.

Another task is identifying how management will be held accountable for supporting and engaging in those DEIB initiatives. An optional recommended step is creating a diverse committee of employees from all levels with visible leadership presence and support. That committee can be tasked with implementing the goals defined in the previous steps and promoting DEIB in the workplace. The employer should provide the committee with a clear mission or defined budget and expectations and performance indicators.

The diversity committee meets regularly and is typically tasked with the following:

- Responsible for promoting the training and events to bring awareness to DEIB in the workplace.

- Responsible for engaging co-workers and DEIB conversations and training.

- Responsible for reviewing and developing policies and procedures that promote workplace DEIB.

If you do not have a DEIB committee, an employer can also designate responsibility for those tasks to management. They can also consider hiring a DEIB specialist or consultant to help them run that program. The DEIB initiatives may make changes in policies and practices, so staff training, targeted recruiting, and employer-sponsored DEIB awareness events for employees need to be instituted.

An employer may have to develop an action plan to implement these initiatives by setting realistic goals and starting with the elements that have the greatest business value or that are readily achievable to build momentum for the initiative.

Sample DEIB Initiative Action Plan

Objective

To foster a diverse, equitable, and inclusive workplace where all employees feel valued, respected, and empowered to contribute their best.

Timeline

January 2024 - December 2026

Leadership Commitment and Training

- Quarter 1, Year 1: Senior leadership will attend DEIB training to understand the business case for DEIB and the role of leadership in driving change.

- Ongoing: DEIB training will be integrated into leadership development programs to ensure continuous learning and commitment.

DEIB Assessment and Goal Setting

- Quarter 2, Year 1: Conduct a comprehensive DEIB assessment, including surveys and focus groups, to gauge the current state of the organization's diversity and inclusivity.

- Quarter 3, Year 1: Analyze assessment data to set specific and measurable DEIB goals that align with the organization's strategic objectives.

Senior-Level Champion Identification

- Quarter 4, Year 1: Identify a senior-level champion who will be responsible for leading and supporting the DEIB initiative, communicating its importance, and driving its implementation.

Inclusive Recruitment and Hiring

- Year 2: Implement strategies to increase diversity in recruitment and hiring processes, such as creating diverse interview panels, using inclusive language in job postings, and building partnerships with diverse organizations.

Inclusive Workplace Policies and Practices

- Year 2: Review and update HR policies to ensure they are inclusive and equitable, addressing issues such as flexible work arrangements, family support, and accommodations for diverse needs.

Employee Resource Groups (ERGs)

- Year 2: Establish Employee Resource Groups representing diverse communities within the organization to provide support, foster a sense of belonging, and contribute to DEIB initiatives.

Cultural Competency and Unconscious Bias Training

- Year 2: Roll out organization-wide training programs on cultural competency and unconscious bias to increase awareness and promote inclusive behaviors.

Inclusive Leadership Development

- Year 3: Implement leadership development programs that emphasize inclusive leadership practices, empathy, and cross-cultural communication.

Metrics and Accountability

- Ongoing: Develop DEIB Key Performance Indicators (KPIs) to track progress toward goals, regularly report on achievements, and hold leaders accountable for driving DEIB initiatives.

Celebrating Diversity and Inclusion

- Ongoing: Promote diversity celebrations and events to foster a sense of unity and appreciation for the diverse backgrounds and experiences of employees.

Continuous Improvement and Feedback

- Ongoing: Encourage employees to provide feedback on DEIB initiatives and use the insights to continuously improve and adapt strategies.

External Partnerships and Community Engagement

- Year 3: Forge partnerships with external organizations and community groups to enhance DEIB efforts and contribute to broader social impact.

This sample DEIB Initiative Action Plan provides a roadmap for organizations to create a more inclusive workplace. By aligning DEIB initiatives with strategic goals, securing senior-level buy-in, and implementing targeted actions, organizations can build a diverse, equitable, and inclusive culture that supports employee well-being and drives organizational success. Regular monitoring and continuous improvement ensure that the DEIB journey remains dynamic and responsive to the evolving needs of the workforce and the broader community.

Case Study

Building an Equitable Workplace

This case study highlights the transformative journey of a medium-sized consulting firm committed to cultivating a diverse and inclusive workplace. Facing the need for improvement in agency operations, the consulting firm embarked on a comprehensive evaluation process with an equity lens to foster a more equitable and socially responsible work environment. This case study explores the steps taken by the firm to identify and address disparities, the strategies implemented to promote equity, and the positive outcomes achieved through this transformative approach.

The consulting firm prided itself on being an innovative and client-focused organization. However, upon conducting an internal review, the company's leadership acknowledged the potential presence of biases and disparities within their agency operations. Concerns arose regarding the representation of diverse talent at various levels, the lack of inclusive decision-making processes, and potential unconscious biases influencing hiring and promotion decisions. Recognizing the urgency to create a more equitable workplace, the firm is committed to evaluating its agency operations through an equity lens.

Step 1: Equity Assessment and Data Analysis

The firm formed a cross-functional team comprising representatives from different departments to lead the equity assessment process. The team conducted thorough surveys, focus groups, and data analysis to gain a comprehensive understanding of the current state of diversity, inclusion, and representation within the organization. They identified areas of concern, such as gender imbalances in leadership roles and disparities in salary among employees with similar qualifications and experiences.

Step 2: Identifying Equity Gaps and Disparities

Upon analyzing the collected data, the team identified several equity gaps that required immediate attention. The lack of diversity in the leadership team indicated a need for more inclusive promotion practices, while the gender pay gap highlighted the importance of addressing compensation equity. Additionally, feedback from focus groups revealed employees' desire for greater representation and involvement in decision-making processes.

Step 3: Developing an Equity Action Plan

With the insights gained from the assessment, the consulting firm's cross-functional team collaboratively developed a comprehensive equity action plan. The plan included specific and measurable goals, such as achieving gender parity in leadership positions within two years and conducting pay equity audits annually to address salary disparities. To foster inclusivity, the organization established an Employee Resource Group and initiated regular diversity and inclusion training for all employees.

Step 4: Leadership Commitment and Senior-Level Champion

To ensure the success and sustainability of the equity initiatives, the consulting firm's senior leadership team wholeheartedly supported the action plan. They participated in DEIB training and actively championed the importance of equity in agency operations. Furthermore, the consulting firm identified a senior-level champion, the Chief Diversity Officer, to spearhead and oversee the implementation of equity initiatives, ensuring their visibility and continuity.

Step 5: Implementing Equity Initiatives

With the equity action plan in place, the consulting firm embarked on implementing the proposed initiatives. Hiring practices were revised to ensure a diverse candidate pool and structured mentorship programs were introduced to support the advancement of underrepresented groups. Additionally, employee performance evaluations incorporated considerations for inclusive leadership behaviors, encouraging managers to embrace diversity in their teams actively.

Outcomes and Impact

Over the course of three years, the consulting firm witnessed significant positive outcomes from its equity initiatives. The proportion of women in leadership roles increased by 30%, and the gender pay gap was narrowed by 15%. Employee satisfaction and engagement improved as individuals felt more included and valued within the organization. Additionally, client feedback highlighted the positive impact of diverse perspectives on the quality and innovation of services provided by the consulting firm.

Conclusion

The consulting firm's case study exemplifies the importance of evaluating agency operations with an equity lens to foster a diverse and inclusive workplace culture. By committing to data-driven assessments, identifying equity disparities, and developing a comprehensive action plan, the organization achieved positive and sustainable outcomes. Through senior-level buy-in and the dedication of a champion, the consulting firm established a new standard for equitable agency operations, creating a workplace environment that celebrates diversity and empowers all employees to thrive. The success of this transformation serves as an inspiration for other organizations seeking to build a more inclusive and socially responsible workplace.

Integrative Exercise

Assessing Operations through an Equity Lens

The following exercise is designed to help organizations assess their agency operations through an equity lens. It aims to promote understanding, collaboration, and actionable insights for fostering a more inclusive and equitable workplace environment. This exercise can be completed in a half-day workshop or over multiple sessions, depending on the organization's size and complexity of operations.

Materials Needed

- Whiteboard or flipchart

- Markers and sticky notes

- Handouts on equity principles and relevant agency data (if available)

Step 1: Introducing Equity Principles

Begin by introducing the concept of equity and its relevance in agency operations. Provide an overview of the key principles of equity, such as fairness, inclusivity, and eliminating disparities.

Encourage participants to share their understanding of equity and any relevant experiences they have had with implementing equity initiatives in the workplace.

Step 2: Mapping Agency Operations

Divide participants into small groups, each focusing on a specific area of agency operations, such as hiring, promotions, training, or decision-making processes.

Ask each group to map out the current processes and practices in their assigned area. This can be done using a flowchart or a step-by-step description.

As a facilitator, guide the groups to identify potential areas where equity concerns may arise, such as bias in hiring criteria or lack of diversity in decision-making committees.

Step 3: Equity Impact Assessment

Have each group analyze the mapped processes and discuss the potential impact of these practices on different groups within the organization. Encourage discussions on how certain practices may disproportionately affect certain demographics.

Facilitate a discussion on the significance of addressing equity concerns and the benefits of fostering a more inclusive workplace.

Step 4: Data Analysis and Identifying Disparities

Provide relevant agency data on demographics, representation, and workforce diversity, if available. If not, encourage participants to brainstorm data that would be useful for assessing equity in agency operations.

Ask participants to analyze the data and identify any disparities or patterns related to representation, promotion rates, pay gaps, or other indicators of equity.

Step 5: Developing Equity Action Plans

Reassemble the larger group and have each small group present their findings and insights from Steps 2, 3, and 4.

Facilitate a collaborative discussion to identify specific areas of improvement and strategies for addressing the identified equity concerns. Encourage participants to think creatively and suggest practical solutions.

Have each group develop an equity action plan with clear goals, timelines, responsible parties, and evaluation measures.

Step 6: Sharing and Committing to Equity Initiatives

Have each group share their equity action plans with the entire organization. This can be done through presentations or poster displays.

As a closing activity, ask participants to individually commit to supporting and actively participating in the implementation of the proposed equity initiatives.

This integrative exercise empowers organizations to evaluate their agency operations through an equity lens and identify opportunities for improvement. By collaboratively developing actionable equity action plans, participants commit to creating a workplace environment that values diversity, promotes inclusivity, and fosters equal opportunities for all. The exercise provides a solid foundation for ongoing efforts to build a more equitable and socially responsible organization.

Chapter Ten

Evaluating Board Operations through an Equity Lens

I n this chapter, we explore the critical importance of evaluating board operations through an equity lens. Boards of directors play a pivotal role in guiding organizations, setting strategic direction, and making critical decisions. By examining board operations with an inclusive perspective, organizations can identify potential biases, disparities, and opportunities to foster greater diversity, equity, and inclusion at the highest level of leadership.

Understanding the Equity Lens for Board Evaluations

We begin by defining the equity lens and its significance in the context of board evaluations. The equity lens challenges traditional norms and biases that may hinder diversity and inclusivity within boards. We explore the potential impact of inclusive board practices on organizational performance, reputation, and stakeholder trust.

The equity lens, in the context of board evaluations, refers to an approach that assesses board performance and composition through the lens of equity, diversity, and inclusion. It involves scrutinizing board processes, policies, and decision-making to identify and rectify any biases or barriers that may hinder the representation of diverse perspectives and experiences within the boardroom. The primary goal of applying the equity lens is to create a more inclusive and representative board that reflects the broader demographic and social diversity of the organization's stakeholders and the society at large.

The significance of the equity lens in board evaluations lies in its potential to challenge traditional norms and biases that have historically limited access and opportunities for underrepresented groups. By doing so, it can help break down barriers and foster a more inclusive and equitable corporate culture.

Here are some key points to consider regarding its significance:

- **Promoting Diversity and Inclusion:** An equitable board evaluation process encourages the inclusion of individuals from diverse backgrounds, including but not limited to gender, race, ethnicity, age, nationality, sexual orientation, and socio-economic status. A more diverse board brings a variety of perspectives, ideas, and experiences to the decision-making process, leading to better-informed and more innovative outcomes.

- **Enhanced Organizational Performance:** Studies have shown that diverse and inclusive boards can positively impact organizational performance. A board with diverse members is better equipped to understand and respond to the needs of an increasingly diverse customer base. Different viewpoints and expertise can lead to more effective risk management, strategic planning, and problem-solving, ultimately driving better business performance.

- **Reputation and Stakeholder Trust:** An organization that prioritizes diversity and inclusion at the board level is likely to earn the trust and respect of its stakeholders. This includes employees, customers, investors, regulators, and the broader community. Such trust is invaluable and can positively influence an organization's reputation and long-term sustainability.

- **Reducing Groupthink and Bias:** An equitable evaluation process challenges groupthink, a phenomenon where individuals in a cohesive group tend to conform to prevailing opinions and limit dissenting viewpoints. By fostering a diverse board, the equity lens can help mitigate the risk of biased decision-making and encourage more robust discussions and critical analysis.

- **Compliance and Corporate Governance:** In some regions, there are legal and regulatory requirements related to board diversity and corporate governance. Applying an equity lens to board evaluations can ensure that an organization remains compliant with these regulations and fosters a culture of ethical leadership and responsible corporate citizenship.

- **Talent Attraction and Retention:** Organizations that demonstrate a commitment to diversity and inclusion are more likely to attract and retain top talent. Diverse individuals seeking leadership positions are more inclined to join companies that prioritize equity, knowing their contributions will be valued and respected.

In conclusion, the equity lens is a powerful tool that challenges traditional norms and biases, promoting diversity, inclusivity, and better decision-making within corporate boards. Embracing an equitable evaluation process can have a significant positive impact on organizational performance, reputation, and stakeholder trust, creating a more sustainable and successful company overall.

Reviewing Board Composition and Diversity

In this section, we delve into the importance of board composition and the representation of diverse voices. We examine the benefits of diverse perspectives in decision-making processes and how a broad range of backgrounds can enrich board discussions. Practical methods for assessing and enhancing board diversity are discussed.

Board composition and diversity play a crucial role in the effective functioning of any organization. A well-structured and diverse board can bring a wealth of benefits, positively impacting decision-making processes and overall governance.

Let us explore the key points to consider when reviewing board composition and diversity.

- **Importance of Diverse Perspectives:** A board that includes individuals from diverse backgrounds, experiences, and expertise can offer a wide range of perspectives on various issues. This diversity helps avoid groupthink and fosters creative problem-solving. When faced with complex challenges, diverse boards can consider a broader array of solutions, leading to more robust and innovative decisions.

- **Enhanced Decision Making:** Board diversity brings together people with unique insights into the concerns and needs of different stakeholders, such as customers, employees, and communities. This comprehensive understanding allows the board to make decisions that consider a broader spectrum of interests, leading to more sustainable and inclusive outcomes.

- **Improved Corporate Governance:** Diverse boards are more likely to uphold transparency and accountability, as they inherently represent a wider range of stakeholders' interests. This can contribute to a higher level of trust and confidence from shareholders and the public.

- **Enhanced Board Dynamics:** When individuals from various backgrounds collaborate on a board, it can lead to a more dynamic and stimulating boardroom environment. Diverse perspectives can challenge assumptions, promote constructive debates, and prevent homogeneity-driven complacency.

- **Practical Methods for Assessing Diversity:** To assess board diversity, organizations can consider factors such as gender, ethnicity, age, professional expertise, and geographic representation of board members. Regular evaluations of board composition help identify gaps and opportunities for improvement.

- **Challenges in Achieving Diversity:** Despite the recognized benefits of diversity, some challenges may hinder achieving it. These challenges can include unconscious biases during the recruitment process, a limited pool of diverse candidates with board experience, and resistance to change within the organization.

- **Methods to Enhance Board Diversity:** Organizations can take proactive steps to enhance board diversity. These methods may include setting diversity targets or quotas, establishing inclusive recruitment practices, providing board training on diversity and inclusion, and fostering a culture that values diverse perspectives.

- **Stakeholder Engagement:** Engaging with stakeholders can help identify and address concerns regarding board diversity. Organizations can seek feedback from shareholders, employees, customers, and the broader community to understand their expectations regarding board representation.

In conclusion, board composition and diversity are crucial elements that can significantly impact an organization's success and governance. Embracing diverse voices and experiences within the boardroom can lead to more effective decision-making, improved corporate governance, and ultimately, better outcomes for all stakeholders involved. By actively assessing and enhancing board diversity, organizations can create a more inclusive and forward-thinking governance structure.

Assessing Decision-Making Processes

Effective decision-making is essential for board success. Here, we analyze board decision-making processes through an equity lens. We explore the role of unconscious biases and potential barriers that may prevent the equitable consideration of all viewpoints. Strategies for promoting inclusive decision-making are examined.

Analyzing board decision-making processes through an equity lens is a critical step toward ensuring fair and inclusive outcomes. Effective decision-making is essential for boards to fulfill their responsibilities and achieve organizational success.

Let us break down the key components involved in this analysis:

- **Unconscious Biases:** Unconscious biases are implicit preferences or attitudes that individuals hold towards certain groups or characteristics. These biases can influence decision-making, often leading to unfair treatment or exclusion of certain viewpoints. In a board setting, unconscious biases may affect how certain ideas or suggestions are perceived and considered, potentially hindering equitable decision-making.

- **Barriers to Equitable Consideration:** There are various barriers that may impede the equitable consideration of all viewpoints during board decision-making. These barriers could include a lack of diversity in the boardroom, hierarchical power structures, and groupthink. When board members come from similar backgrounds or have similar perspectives, it can be challenging to ensure that all voices are heard and that decisions reflect the needs and concerns of a diverse stakeholder base.

- **Promoting Inclusive Decision-Making Strategies:** To address these challenges and promote inclusive decision-making, several strategies can be employed:

  - *Diversity and Inclusion Initiatives:* Boards should actively work to diversify their membership by seeking individuals with diverse backgrounds, experiences, and perspectives. Inclusive decision-making benefits from a wide range of viewpoints and insights.

  - *Training and Awareness:* Board members and executives should receive training to recognize and mitigate unconscious biases. Raising awareness of these biases can help individuals make more conscious and equitable decisions.

  - *Open Dialogue and Psychological Safety:* Fostering an environment of open dialogue where all members feel psychologically safe to express their opinions without fear of retribution is crucial. This encourages the sharing of diverse viewpoints and dissenting opinions.

  - *Decision-Making Frameworks:* Implementing structured decision-making frameworks can help reduce the influence of biases. Objective criteria and data-driven approaches can guide the decision-making process and minimize the impact of personal preferences.

  - *External Review and Feedback:* Boards can seek external input or conduct third-party assessments of their decision-making processes. External perspectives can offer valuable insights and identify potential blind spots.

  - *Monitoring and Evaluation:* Regularly monitoring and evaluating board decisions and their impact can help identify patterns of bias and inform ongoing efforts to improve the decision-making process.

By actively incorporating these strategies, boards can enhance their decision-making processes and move towards more equitable and inclusive outcomes. This, in turn, can lead to better organizational performance and stronger stakeholder trust. It is important to recognize that promoting inclusive decision-making is an ongoing process that requires continuous effort and commitment from all board members and stakeholders.

Addressing Power Dynamics

Addressing power dynamics within boards is crucial for promoting inclusivity and ensuring that all board members can effectively contribute and participate in decision-making processes. Power imbalances can lead to certain voices being marginalized or silenced, hindering the board's ability to make well-rounded and informed decisions.

Here are some strategies to foster inclusivity and create an empowering environment on the board:

- **Diverse Representation:** Actively seek to create a diverse board with members from diverse backgrounds, experiences, and perspectives. Having a variety of viewpoints at the table helps challenge assumptions and avoids groupthink.

- **Inclusive Leadership:** Board leaders should be mindful of their role in encouraging participation and ensuring that all voices are heard. They can set the tone for open discussions and demonstrate their commitment to inclusivity through their actions.

- **Establish Ground Rules:** Develop and communicate clear ground rules for board meetings that emphasize mutual respect, active listening, and equal opportunities for speaking. Encourage constructive dissent and debate while discouraging any form of discrimination or disrespect.

- **Active Listening:** Board members must actively listen to each other, allowing everyone to finish their thoughts without interruption. Active listening involves genuinely considering and valuing the input of others.

- **Rotate Facilitation:** Consider rotating the role of the meeting facilitator to avoid a single individual dominating the discussion. This practice can help distribute power and encourage different leadership styles.

- **Anonymity for Ideas:** In certain situations, such as brainstorming sessions, consider using anonymous idea-sharing methods to encourage more reserved members to contribute without fear of judgment.

- **Mentorship and Support:** Foster mentorship programs where experienced board members can support and encourage newer or less confident members to express their opinions and ideas.

- **Training and Workshops:** Offer training sessions and workshops on communication, diversity, and inclusion. These initiatives can help board members develop the necessary skills and awareness to navigate power dynamics and promote inclusivity effectively.

- **Regular Evaluations:** Conduct regular evaluations of board dynamics, including feedback on the board's inclusivity. Use the insights gained to make continuous improvements.

- **External Facilitators:** In situations where existing power dynamics are particularly entrenched, bringing in an external facilitator to conduct meetings can provide a neutral and unbiased perspective, helping to level the playing field.

- **Transparency and Information Sharing:** Ensure that all board members have access to relevant information in a timely manner. Transparency in decision-making processes reduces the likelihood of information being used as a tool to consolidate power.

- **Recognize and Address Biases:** Encourage board members to be aware of their biases and to challenge them actively. Establish a culture where feedback regarding potential bias is welcomed and used as an opportunity for growth.

- **Celebrate Contributions:** Recognize and celebrate the contributions of all board members. Acknowledge their efforts and value their unique perspectives.

By implementing these strategies, boards can create an inclusive environment where all members feel empowered to voice their opinions and contribute meaningfully. Embracing diversity and addressing power dynamics fosters a more productive and effective board that can make well-informed decisions for the betterment of the organization or community they serve.

Case Study

Fostering Inclusivity on the Nonprofit Board

A nonprofit organization was dedicated to empowering underprivileged youth through education and mentorship programs. The organization had been making a significant impact in the community for several years. However, the board of directors noticed that certain power dynamics and communication issues were affecting decision-making and the overall inclusivity of the board. They realized the importance of addressing these challenges to ensure all board members could contribute meaningfully to the organization's mission.

Case Study Details

- **Board Composition:** The nonprofit board was composed of twelve members, each with diverse backgrounds and expertise. However, a closer examination reveals that the majority of the board members come from similar professional backgrounds, leading to a potential bias in decision-making and communication styles.

- **Dominant Voices:** During board meetings, a few individuals tend to dominate discussions while others remain more reserved. Some board members have expressed feeling intimidated or unheard, which hinders their ability to contribute their ideas and perspectives fully.

- **Lack of Inclusive Decision-Making:** In the past, certain significant decisions were made without engaging all board members equally in the process. This lack of inclusive decision-making has led to feelings of exclusion among some members, resulting in reduced engagement and enthusiasm.

- **Unclear Ground Rules:** Board meetings lack established ground rules for communication and participation, leading to confusion about the expectations for behavior during discussions.

- **Impact on Board Culture:** The existing power dynamics and communication challenges led to a less cohesive board culture. The lack of inclusivity had also affected collaboration among board members, potentially hindering the organization's progress.

Strategies for Fostering Inclusivity

- **Diverse Representation:** The board acknowledged the importance of having diverse perspectives to improve decision-making. They actively sought new board members from various professional backgrounds and life experiences to create a more representative and inclusive board.

- **Active Listening Training:** The board organized a training workshop on active listening and effective communication. The workshop helped board members understand the impact of their communication styles and provides practical techniques to promote active listening and empathy.

- **Establishing Ground Rules:** In collaboration with all board members, the board developed a set of ground rules for board meetings. These rules emphasize the value of all perspectives and set expectations for respectful communication, active participation, and constructive dissent.

- **Rotating Facilitation:** To distribute power and encourage equal participation, the board introduced a rotating facilitation system.

Each member took turns leading the board meetings, ensuring that different leadership styles were embraced and that everyone has the opportunity to guide discussions.

- **Anonymous Idea-Sharing:** During brainstorming sessions, the board adopted an anonymous idea-sharing method. Board members were encouraged to submit ideas and suggestions without revealing their identities. This approach empowered quieter members to contribute freely without fear of judgment or criticism.

- **Mentorship Program:** The board established a mentorship program where experienced board members were paired with newer or less confident members. Mentors provided guidance and support, helping their mentees feel more comfortable expressing their opinions and contributing to discussions.

Results and Impact

As a result of these strategies, the nonprofit board experienced positive changes in their dynamics and inclusivity:

- Board members from diverse backgrounds brought fresh perspectives to decision-making, resulting in more innovative and effective strategies for the organization's initiatives.

- The rotating facilitation system encourages active participation from all board members and ensures that no single individual dominates discussions.

- Ground rules for board meetings created a more respectful and inclusive environment, enabling all board members to feel valued and heard.

- The mentorship program fostered stronger relationships among board members, promoting a supportive and collaborative board culture.

- Anonymous idea-sharing allows for more creative input and encourages all members to share their ideas without hesitation.

Through their commitment to addressing power dynamics and promoting inclusivity, the nonprofit board successfully created an empowering environment where all members felt encouraged to voice their opinions and contribute meaningfully to the organization's mission. By continuously implementing these strategies, the board ensured that inclusivity remained a core value, driving the nonprofit's continued success in empowering underprivileged youth in the community.

Integrative Exercise

Building an Inclusive Board Culture

In this exercise, you will take on the role of a board member or facilitator tasked with fostering inclusivity and addressing power dynamics within your organization's board. You will work through various scenarios and challenges that commonly arise in board meetings to create a more empowering and open environment. This exercise is designed to integrate the knowledge and strategies discussed earlier. Feel free to involve other board members or colleagues to make it a collaborative experience.

Step 1: Setting the Stage

Imagine that your organization has recognized the importance of promoting inclusivity within the board and has appointed you to lead efforts in this area. Gather information about the current board dynamics, including any perceived power imbalances or challenges faced by certain members in expressing their ideas.

Step 2: Board Evaluation and Goal Setting

Conduct a thorough evaluation of the board's inclusivity and power dynamics. You can use surveys, individual interviews, or a combination of both to gather insights from board members. Based on the findings, set specific and measurable goals for creating a more inclusive board culture.

Step 3: Training and Workshop

Organize a training session or workshop for all board members focused on communication, diversity, and inclusion. Collaborate with experts if needed, and design interactive activities to help board members identify their biases and develop active listening skills. Encourage open discussions during the workshop to foster a sense of camaraderie and shared responsibility.

Step 4: Establish Ground Rules

With input from the board members, establish a set of ground rules for board meetings that emphasize mutual respect, equal participation, and active listening. Display these rules prominently in the meeting room as a visual reminder.

Step 5: Rotate Facilitation

Introduce the concept of rotating facilitation during board meetings. Encourage board members to take turns leading the meetings to distribute power and encourage different leadership styles. Support less experienced facilitators by providing tips and feedback.

Step 6: Anonymous Idea-Sharing

In your next brainstorming session, implement an anonymous idea-sharing method. This can be done by using digital tools or simply collecting written suggestions without attributing them to individuals. This exercise encourages quieter members to contribute freely without fear of judgment.

Step 7: Mentorship Program

Create a mentorship program where experienced board members are paired with newer or less confident members. The mentors can offer guidance, support, and encouragement to help their mentees feel more comfortable expressing their opinions.

Step 8: Regular Check-Ins and Evaluation

Schedule regular check-ins with the board to discuss progress toward the inclusivity goals and gather feedback on the effectiveness of the strategies implemented. Make adjustments and improvements based on the feedback received.

Step 9: Recognize and Celebrate Contributions

Acknowledge and celebrate the contributions of all board members during meetings. Take a moment to highlight specific instances where different perspectives have led to better decisions or outcomes.

Step 10: Ongoing Commitment

Ensure that the efforts to promote inclusivity and address power dynamics remain a continuous and integral part of the board's culture. Incorporate these principles into board orientations for new members and emphasize their importance during board retreats or strategic planning sessions.

After implementing the above strategies over a few months, take some time to reflect on the changes you have observed in the board's dynamics. Evaluate the progress made toward the initial goals and identify areas that may still need improvement. Engage with the board members to gather their feedback and perspectives on the changes. Use this feedback to refine your approach further and continue building a more inclusive and empowering board culture. Remember that inclusivity is an ongoing journey that requires dedication and collective effort.

Chapter Eleven

Nurturing Employee Well-Being and Mental Health through a Holistic Framework

In recent years, there has been a growing recognition of the importance of employee well-being and mental health in the workplace. Employers have come to understand that a happy, healthy, and mentally well workforce is not only more productive but also more loyal and engaged. This shift in perspective has led to a reevaluation of traditional approaches to employee well-being, with many organizations now prioritizing a more holistic approach.

The Importance of Employee Well-Being

Before diving into the details of a holistic approach, it's crucial to understand why employee well-being and mental health matter. Employees are the heart of any organization, and their well-being directly impacts the success of the business.

Here are some key reasons why prioritizing employee well-being is essential:

- **Productivity and Performance:** Employees who are physically and mentally healthy are more likely to be productive and perform at their best. They can concentrate better, make fewer errors, and handle stress more effectively.

- **Retention:** Organizations that invest in employee well-being are more likely to retain their top talent. High turnover rates can be costly, both in terms of recruitment and lost knowledge.

- **Engagement:** Well-being is closely linked to employee engagement. Engaged employees are enthusiastic about their work, feel a sense of purpose, and are more likely to go the extra mile.

- **Innovation:** A workforce that is mentally and physically well is more likely to be innovative. They have the mental space to think creatively and come up with new ideas.

- **Company Reputation:** A commitment to employee well-being can enhance a company's reputation, making it more attractive to both customers and potential employees.

The Holistic Approach to Employee Well-Being

A holistic approach to employee well-being recognizes that well-being encompasses physical, mental, emotional, and even social aspects. It goes beyond traditional wellness programs and looks at the whole person.

Here are the key components of a holistic approach:

- **Physical Health:** Encourage physical well-being through initiatives like gym access, healthy food options, and regular health check-ups. Consider flexible work hours to accommodate exercise routines and promote a healthy work-life balance.

- **Mental Health:** Mental health is a critical component of well-being. Provide resources such as employee assistance programs (EAPs), access to mental health professionals, and destigmatize mental health discussions in the workplace.

- **Work-Life Balance:** Promote a healthy work-life balance by setting clear boundaries, discouraging excessive overtime, and allowing employees to take time off when needed. Encourage managers to lead by example in this regard.

- **Emotional Well-Being:** Create a supportive and empathetic workplace culture where employees feel safe discussing their emotions and seeking help when needed. Offer training to employees and managers on emotional intelligence and communication.

- **Social Connections:** Foster social connections among employees through team-building activities, social events, and creating spaces for collaboration. Strong social bonds can improve overall well-being.

- **Financial Wellness:** Provide resources and education on financial wellness, including budgeting, saving, and retirement planning. Financial stress can significantly impact mental and emotional well-being.

- **Professional Development:** Offer opportunities for skill development and career advancement. When employees feel like they are growing and progressing, it positively affects their overall well-being.

- **Recognition and Appreciation:** Recognize and appreciate employees' efforts and achievements regularly. Feeling valued at work contributes to a positive sense of self-worth.

Implementing a Holistic Approach

Implementing a holistic approach to employee well-being requires commitment and effort at all levels of an organization.

Here are some steps to get started:

- **Leadership Buy-In:** Leadership must be committed to prioritizing employee well-being and set an example for the rest of the organization.

- **Assessment:** Conduct surveys and assessments to understand the specific well-being needs and concerns of your employees. Use this data to tailor your well-being programs.

- **Education and Training:** Train managers and employees on the importance of well-being and how to support each other.

- **Programs and Policies:** Develop and implement well-being programs and policies that address the holistic needs of employees.

- **Regular Evaluation:** Continuously evaluate the effectiveness of your well-being initiatives and make adjustments as needed.

- **Promote Work-Life Integration:** Encourage employees to integrate their work and personal lives in a way that works for them. Flexibility can be a powerful tool in this regard.

- **Open Communication:** Create channels for open communication where employees can voice their concerns or seek help without fear of reprisal.

I once worked for an organization that for years had been a pioneer in its industry, known for its cutting-edge products and technological advancements. However, beneath the surface, the company faced a growing problem: employee burnout and dissatisfaction were on the rise. The company's CEO was a visionary leader who recognized that something needed to change. She hired me as a consultant, due to my expertise in employee well-being and holistic workplace transformations.

I arrived at the organization and immediately began to assess the situation. I interviewed employees from all levels of the organization, from engineers and developers to administrative staff and managers. What I discovered was a company with immense potential but an increasingly stressed and disengaged workforce.I decided to weave my findings into a compelling story for the CEO and the executive team, illustrating the impact of a holistic approach to well-being. I shared the story of a talented software engineer who had been with the organization for five years.

This employee was a rising star in the company, known for their innovative solutions and tireless work ethic. However, behind their impeccable code and consistent late-night shifts, they were struggling. They rarely took breaks, hardly saw their friends or family, and were perpetually exhausted.

One day, this employee's physical health began to deteriorate due to the constant stress and lack of self-care. They were diagnosed with a severe case of burnout and had to take an extended leave of absence. The organization not lost not only their expertise but also the morale of their team, who felt overwhelmed without their leader's guidance.

I continued the story, illustrating how this employee's experience was not unique within the company. There were countless employees who, like her, were silently suffering, leading to decreased productivity, increased absenteeism, and a general sense of discontentment. But the story didn't end there. I painted a vivid picture of a transformed organization.

With my guidance, the company implemented a holistic approach to well-being:

- They introduced flexible work arrangements, allowing employees to tailor their schedules to their needs.

- The organization invested in wellness programs, including yoga classes, mental health workshops, and nutrition counseling.

- Managers received training in emotional intelligence and effective communication to better support their teams.

- A culture of recognition and appreciation was nurtured, boosting employee morale.

As a result, the employee returned to the organization feeling rejuvenated and supported. She became an advocate for the well-being initiatives, leading her team by example. Productivity soared, absenteeism decreased, and the once-disconnected workforce began to bond over shared wellness activities. The CEO, inspired by my storytelling, fully embraced the holistic approach to well-being. The organization became a beacon of employee satisfaction and innovation. They even extended their influence by sharing their journey, inspiring other companies to prioritize employee well-being.

The story of this organization serves as a testament to the transformative power of prioritizing holistic well-being in the workplace. It reminds us that behind every employee is a unique story, and by caring for their physical, mental, emotional, and social well-being, organizations can unlock their full potential and thrive in harmony.

Case Study

The Holistic Well-Being Transformation

A rapidly growing tech company was grappling with a problem common in many modern workplaces: employee burnout, disengagement, and high turnover. Despite its impressive financial growth, the organization's leadership recognized the need for a holistic well-being transformation. This case study explores how they successfully implemented a comprehensive well-being program, emphasizing the physical, mental, emotional, and social health of their employees.

Background

The company was founded a decade ago and has achieved remarkable success in the highly competitive tech industry. However, this success came at a cost: employee stress levels were soaring, absenteeism was on the rise, and the organization was struggling to retain its top talent.

The Challenge

- **High Turnover:** The company was experiencing higher-than-average turnover rates, particularly among its most talented employees. Replacing and retraining staff was expensive and disrupted workflow.

- **Burnout and Disengagement:** An overworked and disengaged workforce led to decreased productivity and a lack of innovation. Employee morale was at an all-time low.

- **Healthcare Costs:** The company's healthcare expenses were steadily increasing due to stress-related health issues among employees.

The Solution

The company took a proactive approach to address these challenges by implementing a holistic well-being program.

Key Components of the Program

- **Physical Well-Being**

    - Gym access and fitness classes at the workplace.

    - Ergonomic workstations to promote good posture.

    - Encouragement of regular breaks to combat sedentary behavior.

- **Mental Health Support**

    - Employee Assistance Program (EAP) provides counseling and resources.

    - Stress management workshops and mindfulness training.

    - Encouraging open discussions about mental health to reduce stigma.

- **Emotional Well-Being**

    - Leadership training in emotional intelligence.

    - Promotion of a positive workplace culture that fosters emotional expression and support.

    - Regular recognition and appreciation of employee contributions.

- **Social Connections**

  - Team-building activities and events.

  - Mentorship programs to encourage social interactions.

  - A collaborative workspace design to facilitate communication and teamwork.

Implementation

The company rolled out the well-being program over the course of a year, starting with leadership training and gradually introducing various components. They actively involved employees in the process, seeking feedback and adjusting the program accordingly.

Results

- **Reduced Turnover:** Employee turnover decreased by 25% within the first year of the program's implementation. Top talent began to stay with the company, contributing to organizational stability.

- **Increased Productivity:** Employee engagement scores rose, and the company experienced a noticeable uptick in productivity and innovation. Teams began to collaborate more effectively, leading to the development of several successful projects.

- **Healthcare Savings:** Healthcare costs decreased by 15% as employees reported fewer stress-related health issues and better overall health.

- **Positive Culture:** The organization's culture became more positive, characterized by open communication, support, and a sense of community among employees.

The holistic well-being transformation at the company demonstrated that prioritizing employee well-being in all its facets is not only ethically responsible but also strategically beneficial. By investing in physical, mental, emotional, and social well-being, the company not only improved the quality of life for its employees but also achieved significant improvements in retention rates, productivity, and healthcare costs. This case study serves as an example of how a holistic approach to employee well-being can drive positive change and success in the modern workplace.

Integrative Exercise

Well-Being Wheel

The objective of this integrative exercise is to help participants assess and enhance their holistic well-being across various dimensions, including physical, mental, emotional, and social aspects.

Materials Needed

- Whiteboard or flip chart

- Markers

- Handouts with the Well-Being Wheel diagram (a circle divided into sections representing different aspects of well-being)

Step 1: Introduction (10 minutes)

- Begin by introducing the concept of holistic well-being, explaining that it encompasses physical, mental, emotional, and social dimensions.

- Share the Well-Being Wheel diagram with the participants and briefly explain the different sections representing each aspect of well-being.

Step 2: Self-Assessment (15 minutes)

- Distribute the Well-Being Wheel handouts to each participant. Ask them to take a few minutes to individually assess their current well-being in each dimension by rating themselves on a scale from

1 (low) to 10 (high) within each section of the wheel.

- Once participants have completed their self-assessment, encourage them to reflect on their ratings and identify areas where they would like to improve.

Step 3: Group Discussion (20 minutes)

- Facilitate a group discussion by asking participants to share their reflections and insights about their well-being assessments. Encourage open and honest sharing.

- Discuss the importance of balance across all dimensions of well-being and how imbalances can affect overall quality of life and work performance.

Step 4: Goal Setting (15 minutes)

- Transition into goal setting. Ask participants to think about one specific action they can take to improve their well-being in each of the four dimensions (physical, mental, emotional, and social).

- Participants should write down these well-being goals on their handouts.

Step 5: Creating a Plan (15 minutes)

- In pairs or small groups, participants should discuss their goals with each other. Encourage them to share strategies and ideas for achieving their well-being goals.

- Participants should write down any additional strategies or action steps they gather from their group discussions.

Step 6: Sharing and Commitment (10 minutes)

- Invite participants to share one of their well-being goals and the strategies they plan to implement to achieve it with the whole group.

- Emphasize the importance of commitment to these well-being goals and encourage participants to hold each other accountable for their well-being journey.

Step 7: Visualization (10 minutes)

- Conclude the exercise with a brief guided visualization. Ask participants to close their eyes, take deep breaths, and visualize themselves achieving their well-being goals. Encourage them to feel the positive impact of improved well-being in all aspects of their lives.

Step 8: Reflection (10 minutes)

- Finally, ask participants to take a moment to reflect on how this exercise has influenced their perspective on well-being and what steps they will take moving forward.

The Well-Being Wheel exercise is designed to help individuals assess their holistic well-being, set meaningful goals, and develop action plans for improvement. By integrating physical, mental, emotional, and social aspects of well-being, participants can work toward a balanced and fulfilling life both personally and professionally. Encourage participants to revisit their well-being goals regularly and support each other in their well-being journeys.

Chapter Twelve

Leading Organization-Wide DEIB Initiatives

As mentioned in an earlier chapter, the terms Equity, Inclusion, Belonging, and Diversity (EIBD) and Diversity, Equity, Inclusion, and Belonging (DEIB) are often used interchangeably. However, regardless of the order, the principles remain integral to cultivating a truly inclusive and equitable organization.

Some organizations may choose to lead with diversity, placing it at the forefront of their initiatives as a way to address representation and inclusivity from the outset. By prioritizing diversity, these organizations aim to bring a variety of perspectives, backgrounds, and experiences into their workforce, recognizing that a diverse team is often more innovative and better equipped to meet the needs of a global market. However, it's crucial to remember that diversity alone is not enough. Without a simultaneous focus on equity, inclusion, and belonging, efforts to diversify can fall short, potentially leading to tokenism or surface-level changes that don't address deeper systemic issues. Therefore, while leading with diversity is an important step, it must be integrated with comprehensive strategies that ensure all individuals, regardless of their background, have equal access to opportunities, feel included in the organizational culture, and truly belong within the team.

Leading an organization-wide DEIB initiative requires a strategic and holistic approach that permeates every aspect of the organization. This includes embedding DEIB values into the core culture, ensuring tha' all voices are heard and respected, and creating an environment where every individual feels they truly belong. Effective leadership in this area also involves setting clear, measurable goals, providing ongoing education and training, and holding all levels of the organization accountable for progress. By prioritizing DEIB initiatives, organizations can foster a more innovative, engaged, and resilient workforce while positively impacting their broader communities.

Diversity, Equity, Inclusion, and Belonging (DEIB) initiatives have become imperative for organizations in the 21st century. Companies are recognizing that fostering a diverse and inclusive workplace not only aligns with ethical principles but also drives innovation, employee engagement, and overall success. In this chapter, we will explore how to effectively develop, design, and lead an organization-wide DEIB effort.

Establishing a DEIB Vision and Strategy

To create a strong foundation for your organization's DEIB efforts, it's essential to establish a clear vision and strategy.

Here are the key steps involved:

- **Define DEIB Goals:** Begin by clearly defining your organization's DEIB goals. What specific outcomes do you want to achieve? For example, you might aim to increase diversity in leadership positions, reduce turnover among underrepresented groups, or foster a more inclusive workplace culture.

- **Business Rationale:** Clearly articulate why DEIB is essential for your business. Consider the benefits, such as improved innovation, better talent acquisition and retention, enhanced customer relationships, and alignment with ethical values. The business case for DEIB should be compelling and data-driven.

- **Craft a Vision Statement:** Develop a powerful and inspiring DEIB vision statement. This statement should describe the future state of your organization in terms of diversity, equity, inclusion, and belonging. It should reflect your aspirations and set a clear direction for DEIB efforts.

- **Alignment with Values:** Ensure that your DEIB vision aligns with your organization's core values and mission. This alignment reinforces the commitment to DEIB as a fundamental principle.

- **Develop a Comprehensive Plan:** Create a detailed DEIB strategy that outlines the specific steps, initiatives, and resources required to achieve your DEIB goals. This plan should be comprehensive, covering areas such as recruitment, training, policy development, and culture change.

- **Measurable Objectives:** Within your strategy, establish measurable objectives and key performance indicators (KPIs) to track progress. These metrics will help you assess the effectiveness of your DEIB initiatives over time.

- **Resource Allocation:** Determine the resources needed to execute your DEIB strategy successfully. This includes budget allocation, staffing, and technology requirements.

- **Timeline:** Create a timeline with clear milestones and deadlines for your DEIB initiatives. This provides a structured approach to implementation.

Remember that DEIB is an ongoing process that requires commitment and continuous improvement. Regularly revisit your objectives, vision, and strategy to adapt to changing circumstances and evolving best practices. Engage employees at all levels in the process to ensure that your DEIB efforts are inclusive and sustainable.

Gaining Leadership Buy-In

To gain leadership buy-in for your DEIB efforts, it's crucial to engage your organization's top executives effectively. To ensure the success of your DEIB initiatives, you must secure support from senior leadership. It's essential to convince them of the substantial business benefits and the moral imperative of DEIB. Present a compelling case to leadership by highlighting the tangible advantages of DEIB, such as improved innovation, employee engagement, and financial performance. Share industry research and success stories from other organizations that have benefited from robust DEIB programs.

Emphasize the ethical reasons behind DEIB efforts. Explain how fostering a diverse and inclusive workplace aligns with your organization's values and its role in creating a fair and just society. Encourage leaders to reflect on the impact their decisions can have on marginalized groups. Encourage your organization's leaders to actively champion DEIB initiatives by modeling inclusive behavior and participating in DEIB efforts themselves.

Leaders should exemplify inclusive behavior in their interactions with employees, clients, and stakeholders. Demonstrate empathy, active listening, and respect for diverse perspectives. Encourage leaders to actively participate in DEIB initiatives. This might include attending DEIB training sessions, joining employee resource groups (ERGs), or taking a visible role in diversity-related events. Leaders should consistently communicate their commitment to DEIB throughout the organization. Share personal stories or experiences that highlight the importance of diversity and inclusion. This helps create a culture where DEIB is seen as a top organizational priority.

By engaging leadership effectively and encouraging them to become DEIB champions, you'll not only secure their buy-in but also ensure that

DEIB efforts are woven into the fabric of your organization's culture and operations. This top-down support is crucial for the success of organization-wide DEIB initiatives.

Assessing the Current State

Assessing the current state of your organization's DEIB efforts is a critical step in the journey toward creating a more inclusive workplace.

Here are a few key components of this assessment process:

- Begin by gathering comprehensive data on various aspects of your organization's current state with regard to diversity and inclusion. This data serves as a baseline for measuring progress as you implement DEIB initiatives.

- Collect information on the demographics of your workforce, including gender, race, ethnicity, age, disability status, and other relevant categories.

- Analyze these metrics to identify areas where representation may be lacking or where disparities exist.

- Assess the existing workplace culture by examining factors like employee turnover, promotions, and advancement opportunities.

- Look at whether diverse employees have the same access to growth and development as others.

In addition to quantitative data, it's crucial to understand the experiences and perspectives of your employees, especially those from underrepresented groups. This qualitative data provides valuable context and insights.

Here's how to do it:

- Create and administer DEIB-focused surveys that ask employees about their experiences, perceptions, and suggestions related to diversity and inclusion in the workplace. Ensure anonymity to encourage honest responses.

- Organize focus groups comprising employees from diverse backgrounds. Facilitate open discussions about their experiences, challenges, and ideas for improving the workplace climate. These sessions can provide rich, qualitative data.

- Conduct one-on-one interviews with employees, especially those who may have faced barriers or discrimination. These interviews can offer deeper insights into individual experiences and concerns.

By collecting both quantitative and qualitative data through diversity metrics, workplace culture analysis, and employee feedback mechanisms, you'll gain a comprehensive understanding of your organization's current DEIB landscape. This knowledge will serve as a foundation for crafting targeted and effective DEIB strategies and interventions to drive positive change.

Designing Inclusive Policies and Practices

Creating an inclusive workplace involves a critical examination of your organization's policies and practices.

Here are a few key steps in this process:

- **Reviewing Policies:** Begin by evaluating your organization's existing policies, procedures, and practices to identify areas where bias or exclusion may exist.

- **Policy Analysis:** Review all policies related to hiring, promotion, compensation, and employee conduct. Look for any language or practices that could unintentionally disadvantage certain groups. Pay attention to potential biases in recruitment, performance evaluations, and advancement processes.

- **Feedback and Input:** Encourage employees at all levels to provide feedback on policies and practices. Create mechanisms for them to voice concerns or suggest improvements. This can help uncover hidden biases or practices that may inadvertently exclude certain groups.

- **Benchmarking:** Compare your policies and practices to industry best practices and relevant legal requirements. This can help identify gaps and areas where improvements are needed.

- **Training and Development:** Implement training programs to raise awareness about unconscious bias, microaggressions, and inclusivity among employees.

- **Unconscious Bias Training:** Offer training sessions that help employees recognize and address their unconscious biases. These programs aim to increase self-awareness and provide strategies for making fairer decisions.

- **Microaggressions Awareness:** Conduct training on microaggressions, which are subtle, often unintentional, discriminatory actions or comments. Equip employees with tools to respond to and prevent microaggressions in the workplace.

- **Inclusivity Training:** Develop and provide inclusivity training that educates employees on the importance of creating an inclusive environment. This can cover topics such as empathy, active listening, and fostering a culture of respect and belonging.

- **Leadership Training:** Ensure that leadership and management teams receive specialized training in inclusive leadership. Leaders should learn how to model inclusive behaviors, address bias, and champion diversity and inclusion within their teams.

By reviewing and adjusting policies and practices to eliminate bias and promote inclusivity, and by providing training programs that educate employees on these topics, your organization can create a more equitable and welcoming workplace. This not only benefits individual employees but also contributes to improved team dynamics, employee satisfaction, and overall organizational success.

Building a Diverse Workforce

Creating a diverse workforce is a crucial component of a successful DEIB strategy. Key strategies for building and maintaining a diverse workforce include revised recruitment practices, retention strategies, and fostering an inclusive culture.

Revised Recruitment Practices

Begin by revising your recruitment practices to attract diverse talent. This includes:

- **Diverse Hiring Panels:** Form diverse hiring panels that reflect the variety of backgrounds and perspectives you want to attract to your organization. These panels can reduce unconscious bias in the selection process.

- **Alternative Talent Sources:** Expand your search for talent beyond traditional channels. Consider partnerships with diversity-focused job boards, educational institutions, and community organizations. Attend career fairs and networking events that target underrepresented groups.

- **Inclusive Job Descriptions:** Ensure that job descriptions are inclusive and free from biased language. Highlight your organization's commitment to diversity and inclusion in your job postings to signal a welcoming environment.

- **Implicit Bias Training:** Train recruiters and hiring managers on recognizing and mitigating unconscious biases during the hiring process. This training can help ensure that candidates are evaluated fairly based on their qualifications.

Retention Strategies

Retention strategies are vital components of organizational success, particularly in today's competitive and dynamic employment landscape. Effective retention strategies go beyond mere employee satisfaction; they encompass a deliberate effort to understand and meet the needs of employees, fostering a workplace culture where individuals feel valued, engaged, and motivated to contribute their best. By implementing targeted initiatives that prioritize professional development, work-life balance, and inclusive practices, organizations not only enhance employee loyalty but also bolster their reputation as employers of choice. This proactive approach not only reduces turnover but also cultivates a resilient and committed workforce poised for long-term growth and achievement.

Here are some ways to develop retention strategies:

- **Mentorship Programs:** Develop mentorship programs that pair employees from underrepresented groups with more experienced colleagues. Mentorship provides valuable guidance and support for career growth.

- **Employee Resource Groups (ERGs):** Encourage the formation and active participation of ERGs for underrepresented groups. ERGs offer a platform for networking, support, and shared experiences. They can also provide valuable insights to leadership.

- **Career Development Opportunities:** Create career development pathways that offer equal opportunities for advancement to all employees. Ensure that promotions and leadership opportunities are accessible to individuals from diverse backgrounds.

- **Inclusive Policies:** Review and adjust organizational policies to support diversity and inclusion. Policies related to family leave, flexible work arrangements, and accommodations for individuals with disabilities can enhance retention.

- **Regular Feedback and Check-Ins:** Implement regular feedback mechanisms and check-ins with employees to gauge their satisfaction and identify any concerns related to inclusion and career progression.

By revising recruitment practices to attract diverse talent and implementing retention strategies that foster an inclusive and supportive environment, organizations can not only build a diverse workforce but also create an environment where diverse employees thrive and contribute their unique perspectives to the organization's success.

Fostering Inclusive Culture

Creating an inclusive workplace culture requires deliberate efforts and initiatives.

Here are essential strategies to foster inclusivity:

- **Leadership Development:** Invest in leadership development programs that emphasize inclusive leadership skills.

- **Inclusive Leadership Training:** Develop and implement training programs specifically designed for leaders at all levels of your organization. These programs should focus on building inclusive leadership skills, which include empathy, active listening, cultural competence, and the ability to create an environment where diverse perspectives are valued.

- **Accountability:** Hold leaders accountable for creating and maintaining an inclusive workplace. Set clear expectations for inclusive leadership behaviors and evaluate leaders based on their ability to foster diversity and inclusion within their teams.

- **Diverse Leadership:** Encourage diversity in leadership positions. A diverse leadership team can serve as a role model for the entire organization and bring a variety of perspectives to decision-making.

- **Employee Resource Groups (ERGs):** Encourage the formation of ERGs for underrepresented groups, providing a platform for networking and support.

- **Support and Resources:** Provide resources and support for the formation and sustainability of ERGs. This includes allocating budgetary resources, offering meeting spaces, and facilitating communication within and between ERGs.

- **Networking and Professional Development:** Encourage ERGs to host events and activities that promote networking, professional development, and cultural awareness. These groups can provide valuable opportunities for employees to connect, share experiences, and grow in their careers.

- **Executive Sponsorship:** Consider having senior leaders serve as sponsors for ERGs. This can elevate the visibility and importance of these groups within the organization and ensure that their goals align with the broader DEIB strategy.

- **Feedback Mechanisms:** Establish channels for ERGs to provide feedback and recommendations to the organization's leadership. This input can inform DEIB initiatives and policies.

By investing in leadership development programs that prioritize inclusivity and by fostering the creation and growth of ERGs, organizations can create an inclusive culture where all employees feel valued, supported, and empowered to contribute their unique perspectives and talents. This, in turn, enhances employee engagement, creativity, and overall organizational performance.

Measuring and Reporting Progress

To ensure the effectiveness of your DEIB efforts, it's crucial to establish mechanisms for measuring and reporting progress. Two essential strategies to measuring and reporting progress are key performance indicators (KPIs) and regular reporting.

Key Performance Indicators (KPIs)

- **Define Measurable KPIs:** Start by defining specific and measurable Key Performance Indicators (KPIs) that align with your DEIB goals. These KPIs should provide quantitative data that allows you to assess progress accurately. Examples of DEIB KPIs include:

- **Representation Numbers:** Track the diversity of your workforce, especially in leadership positions, by gender, race, ethnicity, age, and other relevant categories.

- **Hiring and Promotion Metrics:** Measure the diversity of candidates in your hiring pipeline and track the rate at which underrepresented employees are promoted to higher roles.

- **Employee Engagement Scores:** Conduct regular surveys to gauge employee engagement and satisfaction, with a specific focus on diversity and inclusion-related questions.

- **Retention Rates:** Monitor turnover rates among underrepresented groups to assess whether your retention strategies are effective.

- **Inclusion Index:** Develop an index that measures the inclusivity of your workplace culture, based on factors like inclusivity training completion rates, employee feedback, and ERG participation.

- **Benchmarking:** Compare your organization's KPIs to industry benchmarks and best practices. This provides context for understanding whether your progress is on par with or surpassing peers in your industry.

Regular Reporting

- **Transparency:** Share DEIB progress and challenges transparently with employees and stakeholders. Transparency builds trust and demonstrates your organization's commitment to DEIB.

- **Regular Updates:** Provide regular updates on your DEIB initiatives and KPIs. These updates can take the form of reports, town hall meetings, newsletters, or dedicated DEIB dashboards accessible to all employees.

- **Action Plans:** When challenges or setbacks are identified, be prepared to communicate action plans for improvement. Demonstrating your organization's commitment to addressing issues is essential.

- **Employee Involvement:** Encourage employees to engage with DEIB reporting by seeking their feedback and input. Actively involve them in the process of evaluating progress and suggesting improvements.

By defining measurable KPIs and regularly reporting on DEIB progress, organizations can track their journey toward a more diverse, equitable, and inclusive workplace. Transparency and accountability are key in driving meaningful change and ensuring that DEIB remains a top priority for the organization.

Adapting and Evolving

Creating a truly inclusive workplace is an ongoing process that requires flexibility and a commitment to continuous improvement.

Here are key principles for adapting and evolving your DEIB efforts:

- **Recognize Ongoing Nature:** Understand that DEIB efforts are not a one-time project; they are an ongoing journey. As circumstances change, so should your strategies and initiatives. Be prepared to continuously assess and refine your DEIB efforts.

- **Regular Reviews:** Schedule regular reviews of your DEIB programs and initiatives. This might be quarterly, annually, or according to your organization's specific needs. These reviews should involve a comprehensive assessment of your KPIs, feedback from employees, and the effectiveness of your strategies.

- **Flexibility:** Be open to adjusting your DEIB strategy in response to new insights, shifts in organizational dynamics, or external factors. Flexibility allows you to adapt your approach to better align with your goals.

- **Innovation:** Encourage innovative thinking in your DEIB efforts. Explore new ways to promote diversity and inclusion, whether it's through technology, partnerships, or creative programs. Encourage employees at all levels to contribute ideas.

- **Learning from Mistakes:** Understand that mistakes are a natural part of any change process, including DEIB initiatives. Embrace a culture where acknowledging and learning from mistakes is encouraged rather than penalized.

- **Root Cause Analysis:** When mistakes occur, conduct a thorough analysis to understand their root causes. This can help you identify systemic issues that may need addressing.

- **Corrective Action:** Take prompt corrective action to rectify mistakes and prevent them from happening again. Communicate these actions transparently to employees and stakeholders.

- **Feedback Loops:** Establish feedback loops that encourage employees to provide input and voice concerns. This feedback can be invaluable in helping your organization learn from mistakes and make improvements.

By recognizing that DEIB efforts are an ongoing process and by learning from mistakes, organizations can create a culture of continuous improvement. This approach ensures that your DEIB initiatives remain responsive to the evolving needs of your workforce and the changing landscape of diversity and inclusion challenges. It also demonstrates your commitment to making meaningful progress in creating a more inclusive workplace.

Developing, designing, and leading an organization-wide DEIB effort is a multifaceted and continuous process. It requires commitment, strategic planning, and a dedication to fostering an inclusive workplace culture. By following the steps outlined in this chapter, organizations can create an environment where diversity is celebrated, equity is promoted, and inclusion is the norm. Ultimately, these efforts will not only benefit employees but also drive organizational success in an increasingly diverse world.

Case Study

Transforming a Company's Diversity and Inclusion Culture

This nonprofit organization is a rapidly growing Human Services company known for its innovative products and services. While the company had achieved success in its industry, it recognized the need to improve its diversity and inclusion efforts. The leadership team understood that a more diverse and inclusive workforce would foster innovation, enhance employee satisfaction, and ultimately drive sustainable growth.

The Challenge

The organization faced several DEIB challenges:

- **Lack of Diversity:** The workforce was predominantly male, with minimal representation from underrepresented groups in leadership roles.

- **Inclusive Culture:** The company's culture was perceived as unwelcoming to diverse employees, with reports of microaggressions and exclusionary behavior.

- **Retention:** There was a high turnover rate among underrepresented employees, which indicated a lack of retention strategies.

- **Measurement and Reporting:** The organization lacked a structured approach to measuring and reporting on DEIB progress, hindering its ability to track improvements and make data-driven decisions.

The Solution

The organization embarked on a comprehensive DEIB transformation journey, including leadership buy-in, assessment, policy review and training, recruitment and retention, culture change, and measurement and reporting.

- **Leadership Buy-In**

  - The CEO and top leadership are championing DEIB efforts, emphasizing the business case for diversity and inclusion.

  - Leadership participates in DEIB training and actively promote an inclusive culture.

- **Assessment**

  - An organization-wide assessment, including surveys, focus groups, and interviews, was conducted to understand the current state of DEIB, employee experiences, and areas needing improvement.

- **Policy Review and Training**

  - HR policies, recruitment practices, and performance evaluation criteria were evaluated and revised to eliminate bias and promote equity.

  - Mandatory unconscious bias training was implemented for all employees and leadership.

- **Recruitment and Retention**

  - Revamped recruitment strategies to attract diverse talent, including using diverse hiring panels and inclusive job descriptions.

- Introduced mentorship programs, Employee Resource Groups (ERGs), and clear career development pathways to retain diverse talent.

- **Culture Change**

  - The organization invested in leadership development programs that emphasized inclusive leadership skills.

  - The formation of ERGs for underrepresented groups, and providing networking and support opportunities was encouraged.

- **Measurement and Reporting**

  - Measurable KPIs, including representation numbers, turnover rates, and an Inclusion Index, were defined to track progress.

  - Regular reporting mechanisms were implemented to share DEIB progress and challenges transparently with employees and stakeholders.

Results

After a year of focused DEIB efforts, The organization saw significant improvements:

- A more diverse workforce, with increased representation from underrepresented groups.

- Reduced turnover among underrepresented employees.

- Improved employee engagement scores, particularly in areas related to diversity and inclusion.

- A more inclusive culture, as evidenced by reduced reports of microaggressions and an increase in ERG participation.

The organization continues its commitment to DEIB, recognizing that it's an ongoing journey requiring continuous improvement, learning from mistakes, and adapting strategies as circumstances evolve. The company's transformation has not only benefited its employees but has also enhanced innovation and competitiveness in the industry.

Integrative Exercises

DEIB Strategy Simulation

The objective of this exercise is to provide participants with hands-on experience in developing, designing, and leading an organization-wide Diversity, Equity, Inclusion, and Belonging (DEIB) strategy. Participants will work in teams to create a DEIB strategy and present their plans, promoting a deeper understanding of the complexities involved in implementing such initiatives.

Materials Needed

- Whiteboard or flip chart with markers.

- DEIB resources (books, articles, guidelines) for reference.

- A list of hypothetical organizations with varying DEIB challenges (prepared in advance).

Step 1: Introduction to DEIB Principles and Challenges (20 minutes)

Start the exercise by providing participants with an overview of DEIB principles and the challenges organizations face when developing, designing, and leading an organization-wide DEIB effort. Use real-world examples and statistics to emphasize the importance of DEIB.

Step 2: Organization Assignment (10 minutes)

Assign each participant or group of participants to a hypothetical organization with specific DEIB challenges. Ensure that each organization has unique characteristics and difficulties related to diversity, equity, inclusion and belonging.

Step 3: Group Brainstorming and Strategy Development (40 minutes)

Participants, grouped by their assigned organizations, will work together to develop a comprehensive DEIB strategy for their respective organizations.

Instruct them to:

- Identify the organization's current DEIB status, including strengths and weaknesses.

- Set clear DEIB objectives and goals.

- Develop a step-by-step action plan outlining specific initiatives, timelines, and resource requirements.

- Consider how to gain leadership buy-in, assess the current state, design inclusive policies, build a diverse workforce, foster an inclusive culture, measure progress, and adapt and evolve.

Step 4: Presentation Preparation (15 minutes)

Each group will prepare a brief presentation of their DEIB strategy. Encourage them to use visual aids, diagrams, and key points to effectively convey their plans.

Step 5: Strategy Presentations (30 minutes)

Each group presents their DEIB strategy to the rest of the participants, explaining the rationale behind their choices and addressing questions from the audience.

Step 6: Group Feedback and Reflection (20 minutes)

After each presentation, facilitate a discussion where other participants provide feedback and suggestions for improvement. Encourage critical thinking and offer guidance on enhancing the presented strategies.

Step 7: Interactive Discussion and Application (15 minutes)

Engage in a group discussion about common themes, best practices, and challenges that emerged during the presentations. Relate these insights to real-life DEIB efforts and encourage participants to think about how they can apply these strategies in their own organizations.

Step 8: Action Planning (20 minutes)

Conclude the exercise by having participants individually or in groups develop an action plan for implementing DEIB initiatives within their own organizations based on what they've learned.

Step 9: Closing Remarks (5 minutes)

Summarize key takeaways from the exercise and emphasize the importance of developing, designing, and leading an organization-wide DEIB effort in today's workplace.

This integrative exercise immerses participants in the process of creating a DEIB strategy for a hypothetical organization, providing a practical understanding of the challenges and considerations involved. It encourages collaboration, critical thinking, and the application of DEIB principles in a real-world context.

Chapter Thirteen

Building Bridges with External Partners

In the pursuit of equity and inclusion, organizations and institutions often find themselves looking beyond their own boundaries. The recognition that promoting equity requires collaboration with external partners has become increasingly evident. This chapter explores the critical importance of building bridges with external partners to extend the reach of equity efforts. We delve into the strategies, challenges, and benefits of such collaborations, highlighting real-world examples to illustrate their transformative potential.

The Imperative for External Partnerships

Equity is not an isolated endeavor. It thrives in environments where diverse voices and perspectives converge, where the power of collective action drives change. External partnerships offer a valuable opportunity to broaden the scope and impact of equity initiatives.

This imperative stems from several key factors:

- **Diverse Expertise:** External partners bring unique knowledge, experiences, and skills to the table. Collaborating with experts from various fields, communities, or industries can enrich your equity initiatives with fresh insights and innovative solutions.

- **Expanded Networks:** Partnering externally broadens your network, connecting you to individuals and groups who share your commitment to equity. These connections can lead to new opportunities for advocacy, resource sharing, and cross-pollination of ideas.

- **Amplified Impact:** Collective efforts often have a more significant impact than solitary ones. Partnering with external organizations or individuals can magnify your reach and influence, making it possible to effect change on a broader scale.

- **Accountability and Oversight:** External partners can serve as a check and balance, holding organizations accountable for their equity commitments. This external scrutiny can help maintain transparency and ensure that equity efforts remain a priority.

Strategies for Building Bridges

Creating meaningful partnerships requires careful planning and a clear understanding of your organization's goals and needs.

Here are some strategies to consider:

- **Define Clear Objectives:** Before seeking external partners, articulate specific equity goals and objectives. Clarify what you hope to achieve through collaboration, whether it's expanding access to education, improving workplace diversity, or addressing systemic inequalities.

- **Identify Compatible Partners:** Look for partners whose values align with your equity mission. Consider organizations, individuals, or communities that have a track record of commitment to similar causes. Compatibility in values and objectives is crucial for a successful partnership.

- **Foster Trust and Mutual Respect:** Building trust is fundamental to any successful partnership. Invest time in developing relationships, actively listening to your partners' perspectives, and demonstrating a genuine commitment to mutual respect and understanding.

- **Share Resources and Expertise:** Partnerships should be mutually beneficial. Share your organization's resources, whether they are financial, human, or intellectual, and leverage the strengths of your partners to achieve your equity goals more effectively.

- **Collaborate on Action Plans:** Work collaboratively to develop action plans that outline roles, responsibilities, and timelines. Ensure that both parties have a clear understanding of how they contribute to the partnership's success.

Real-World Examples

- **Corporate-Community Partnerships:** Many companies are collaborating with local communities to address social and economic disparities. For instance, a technology company might partner with local schools to provide coding workshops and mentorship programs, thereby promoting diversity in the tech industry.

- **Higher Education Consortiums:** Universities often form consortia to share best practices and resources for enhancing diversity and inclusion in higher education. These partnerships facilitate the exchange of ideas and strategies to create more inclusive learning environments.

- **Nonprofit-Government Collaborations:** Nonprofit organizations frequently work with government agencies to advocate for policy changes that promote equity. These partnerships can lead to legislative reforms that address systemic inequalities.

Challenges and Considerations

While external partnerships hold immense potential, they are not without challenges:

- **Power Dynamics:** Navigating power imbalances between partners can be complex. Ensure that equity and fairness are maintained throughout the collaboration, with mechanisms in place to address any issues that arise.

- **Differing Priorities:** Partners may have different priorities and objectives. Effective communication and compromise are essential to ensure that the partnership remains focused on equity goals.

- **Resource Allocation:** Sharing resources and responsibilities can be challenging, especially when partners have limited resources. Clear agreements and ongoing communication are crucial to prevent disputes.

- **Sustainability:** Partnerships should be designed with long-term sustainability in mind. Consider how the collaboration will evolve over time and how to ensure its continuity. Building bridges with external partners is a vital strategy for extending the reach of equity efforts. By embracing diversity, fostering collaboration, and working collectively toward common goals, organizations and institutions can magnify their impact and accelerate progress toward a more equitable and inclusive society. As you embark on this journey, remember that the true power of partnerships lies in the ability to create lasting change that benefits all members of society.

Case Study

The Revival of Main Street

A picturesque small town nestled in the heart of the Midwest faced a common predicament shared by many similar communities across the United States. Its once-thriving Main Street had lost its vitality, with vacant storefronts and a sense of neglect. The town's leaders and community members embarked on a transformative journey to revitalize Main Street, turning it into a vibrant, community-centered hub that would serve as a model for small-town revitalization.

Background

Main Street had been the heartbeat of the town for generations, but in recent years, it had seen a steady decline. The rise of big-box stores on the outskirts of town and shifting consumer preferences had led to a decrease in foot traffic and the closure of several businesses. The community faced economic challenges, including job loss and a declining tax base, which impacted the overall quality of life.

Challenges

- **Economic Decline:** The decline in Main Street's economic activity was a significant concern. The town needed to find a way to attract businesses and visitors back to the area.

- **Infrastructure and Aesthetics:** The aging infrastructure and lack of maintenance had left Main Street with crumbling sidewalks, outdated streetlights, and a general sense of disrepair. This affected the overall appeal of the area.

- **Community Engagement:** Engaging the community in the revitalization efforts was a challenge, as many residents had become disillusioned and skeptical about the possibility of change.

The Transformation

The transformation of Main Street was a multi-faceted endeavor that involved collaboration among various stakeholders, innovative planning, and community engagement.

- **Public-Private Partnership:** Local leaders initiated a public-private partnership that involved collaboration between the town government, local business owners, and community organizations. This partnership allowed for the pooling of resources and expertise to drive the revitalization efforts.

- **Infrastructure and Beautification:** A major part of the transformation involved infrastructure upgrades and beautification. Main Street underwent a comprehensive makeover, with new sidewalks, streetlights, and green spaces. The town also implemented zoning changes to encourage mixed-use development and attract new businesses.

- **Community Engagement:** Engaging the community was essential. The town organized town hall meetings, workshops, and surveys to gather input from residents. This not only provided valuable insights but also instilled a sense of ownership and pride in the revitalization project.

- **Business Incentives:** To attract businesses, the town offered incentives such as tax breaks, low-interest loans, and grants for façade improvements. These incentives were crucial in luring entrepreneurs and investors back to Main Street.

Results

The transformation of Main Street yielded remarkable results:

- **Economic Revival:** Vacant storefronts were replaced with thriving businesses, including boutique shops, cafes, and art galleries. Main Street became a destination for both residents and visitors.

- **Community Pride:** The revitalization efforts instilled a renewed sense of pride and optimism in the community. Residents felt a stronger connection to their town and actively supported local businesses.

- **Increased Property Values:** Property values in the Main Street area increased, leading to higher property tax revenue for the town.

- **Replication:** The town's success story inspired other small towns facing similar challenges to embark on their own revitalization journeys.

Conclusion

The transformation of Main Street demonstrates the power of community collaboration, innovative planning, and community engagement in revitalizing small towns facing economic decline. By addressing economic, aesthetic, and community engagement challenges, the leaders and residents successfully revitalized Main Street, reinvigorating the heart of their town and setting an example for others to follow.

Integrative Exercise

Equity Perspectives Panel Discussion

The objective of this integrative exercise is to promote understanding, empathy, and constructive dialogue around issues of equity, diversity, and inclusion. Participants will engage in a panel discussion format, where they take on the roles of various stakeholders with different perspectives on equity-related topics. This exercise is designed to encourage participants to see issues from multiple angles, foster empathy, and develop collaborative problem-solving skills.

Materials Needed

- Whiteboard or flip chart

- Markers

- Index cards or slips of paper

- Timer or stopwatch

- A list of equity-related topics or scenarios (prepared by the facilitator)

Step 1: Preparation

The facilitator should prepare a list of equity-related topics or scenarios. These could include workplace diversity, educational access, social justice issues, or any other relevant subjects.

Step 2: Setting the Stage

- Begin by explaining the objectives of the exercise: to encourage participants to see issues from various perspectives and foster empathy and constructive dialogue.

- Divide participants into small groups, ideally of 4-6 people each.

- Each group should select a scribe who will jot down key points during the exercise.

- Assign each group a specific equity-related topic or scenario from the prepared list.

Step 3: Panel Discussion One

- Each group will have 20-30 minutes (adjust as needed based on available time) to discuss and prepare for a panel discussion on their assigned topic.

- In each group, participants should take on the roles of different stakeholders who would have varying perspectives on the issue. For example, in a workplace diversity scenario, participants could assume the roles of employees, managers, HR representatives, and community members.

- Encourage participants to think deeply about the concerns, goals, and perspectives of their assigned stakeholder roles. They should prepare key points to present during the panel discussion.

- The scribe in each group should record the main arguments and perspectives discussed.

Step 4: Panel Discussion Two

- Reconvene the whole group and set up a panel discussion format.

- Invite each group to present their topic and the perspectives of the stakeholders they represented. Encourage them to use the whiteboard or flip chart to visually represent key points.

- After each group's presentation, open the floor for questions and comments from the other groups.

- Encourage respectful and empathetic dialogue during the Q&A session.

- Use a timer or stopwatch to ensure that each group's presentation and Q&A session do not exceed a specified time limit (e.g., 10-15 minutes per group).

Step 5: Debrief

- Facilitate a debrief session after all groups have presented and discussed their topics.

- Ask participants to reflect on what they learned from seeing issues from different perspectives.

- Discuss common themes, potential solutions, and ways to bridge gaps in understanding.

- Highlight the importance of empathy and constructive dialogue in addressing equity-related challenges.

Step 6: Conclusion

Conclude the exercise by summarizing key takeaways and emphasizing the value of understanding diverse perspectives when working towards equitable solutions. This integrative exercise not only helps participants gain a deeper understanding of equity-related issues but also enhances their ability to engage in meaningful, empathetic discussions and collaborative problem-solving.

Chapter Fourteen

The Future of Equity in Organizations

I n a world that is rapidly evolving, the concept of equity within organizations has taken on new dimensions and importance. Equity, in the context of workplaces, encompasses fairness, justice, and inclusion, ensuring that every employee has equal access to opportunities and resources, regardless of their background, identity, or circumstances. As we navigate the ever-changing landscape of business, technology, and societal norms, it becomes clear that achieving and maintaining equity is not a static goal but a dynamic process that requires continuous improvement. In this chapter, we will explore the future of equity in organizations and the role of continuous improvement in this journey.

The Changing Landscape of Equity

Equity has long been a cornerstone of modern workplace ideologies. It's not just about adhering to laws and regulations; it's about fostering a culture where diversity is celebrated, and inclusion is the norm. However, the concept of equity is not immune to change.

Equity has evolved in response to various societal and economic shifts:

- **Globalization:** In our interconnected world, organizations must embrace diversity not only within their local communities but also across international borders. The future of equity includes understanding and addressing the unique challenges faced by a globally dispersed workforce.

- **Technology:** Technological advancements have the potential to both enhance and hinder equity. While automation can lead to job displacement, it can also create new opportunities for reskilling and upskilling. Ensuring that these opportunities are accessible to all employees will be a critical aspect of future equity initiatives.

- **Demographic Shifts:** As the workforce becomes more diverse in terms of age, gender, race, and other factors, organizations must adapt to meet the needs and expectations of a broader range of employees. Equity strategies should evolve accordingly.

Continuous Improvement as a Pillar of Equity

Continuous improvement is a philosophy and practice that has long been associated with organizational excellence. Historically, it has been used to optimize processes, reduce waste, and enhance product quality. However, in the future of equity, continuous improvement will play a pivotal role in creating and maintaining inclusive workplaces.

Here's how:

- **Data-Driven Decision-Making:** Continuous improvement relies on data to identify areas for enhancement. In the context of equity, data can illuminate disparities in hiring, promotion, pay, and other critical aspects of the employee experience. Organizations committed to equity will use this data to inform their strategies continually.

- **Feedback Loops:** Continuous improvement thrives on feedback from employees at all levels. In the future, organizations will create feedback mechanisms that allow employees to voice their concerns, suggest improvements, and report incidents of bias or discrimination. These feedback loops will be essential for identifying and rectifying equity-related issues promptly.

- **Learning and Development:** Equity-focused continuous improvement means continuously evolving learning and development programs. Organizations will provide training and resources that promote cultural competency, diversity awareness, and inclusive leadership skills. Regularly updating these programs will be necessary to keep pace with societal changes.

- **Transparent Accountability:** Continuous improvement requires clear accountability. Organizations will establish transparent processes for tracking and reporting progress on equity goals. Leaders will be held responsible for achieving equity-related outcomes, and the results will be shared with employees and stakeholders regularly.

- *Agility and Adaptation:* The future of equity demands organizational agility. Equity challenges can evolve rapidly, and organizations must be prepared to adapt their strategies accordingly. Continuous improvement methodologies provide the flexibility needed to respond to emerging issues effectively.

Strategies for Embracing Continuous Improvement in Equity

To fully embrace continuous improvement in the pursuit of equity, organizations can implement specific strategies.

Strategies for embracing continuous improvement include:

- **Leadership Commitment:** Ensure that top leadership is fully committed to equity as an ongoing priority. Leaders should champion equity initiatives, set an example through their actions, and allocate resources to support continuous improvement efforts.

- **Inclusive Culture:** Foster an inclusive culture where diverse perspectives are valued, and all employees feel safe to express their views. Encourage open dialogue, active listening, and empathy to create an environment where equity can flourish.

- **Regular Audits and Assessments:** Conduct regular equity audits and assessments of policies, practices, and processes. Use the findings to identify areas requiring improvement and to track progress over time.

- **Employee Training and Development:** Continuously update and expand diversity, equity, and inclusion training programs. These programs should address evolving challenges and equip employees with the skills needed to contribute to an inclusive workplace.

- **Inclusive Recruitment and Promotion:** Implement fair and inclusive recruitment and promotion practices. Ensure that biases are minimized throughout the entire talent lifecycle, from job postings to performance evaluations.

- **Feedback Mechanisms:** Establish confidential and accessible channels for employees to provide feedback on equity issues. Use this feedback to identify areas for improvement and celebrate successes.

- **Equity Metrics and Dashboards:** Develop key performance indicators (KPIs) and equity scorecards to monitor progress. Share these metrics with employees and stakeholders to maintain transparency and accountability.

- **Cross-Functional Teams:** Form cross-functional equity teams or committees to drive change collaboratively. These teams can represent various perspectives and work together to develop and implement equity initiatives.

- **Community Engagement:** Engage with external stakeholders, including community organizations and industry groups, to stay informed about best practices, emerging trends, and opportunities for collaboration.

- **Adaptability and Iteration:** Embrace the idea that continuous improvement is an iterative process. Be prepared to adapt strategies and tactics based on the changing needs of the organization and society.

Measuring the Impact of Continuous Improvement in Equity

To measure the impact of continuous improvement efforts in equity, organizations can assess various key indicators, such as:

- **Representation:** Track the diversity of the workforce at all levels, including leadership positions.

- **Pay Equity:** Monitor gender and racial pay gaps and work toward closing them.

- **Employee Satisfaction:** Regularly measure employee

satisfaction, particularly in relation to diversity and inclusion initiatives.

- **Recruitment and Promotion Metrics:** Assess the effectiveness of recruitment and promotion practices in creating diverse talent pipelines.

- **Retention Rates:** Examine turnover rates, especially among underrepresented groups, to identify potential issues.

- **Incident Reporting:** Evaluate the number and nature of equity-related incidents reported and their resolution.

- **Market Reputation:** Assess the organization's reputation in terms of equity and inclusion through surveys and public perception.

- **Supplier Diversity:** Measure the diversity of suppliers and vendors the organization engages with.

The future of equity in organizations is dynamic and ever-evolving. To create and maintain inclusive workplaces, organizations must embrace continuous improvement as a core principle. This means using data, feedback, learning, and transparent accountability to drive progress toward equity goals. It also requires agility and a commitment to adapting strategies as societal and organizational landscapes change.

Embracing continuous improvement in the pursuit of equity is not just a response to changing times; it is an investment in the long-term success and sustainability of organizations. By committing to ongoing assessment, adaptation, and innovation, organizations can create environments where every individual has the opportunity to thrive. The future of equity in organizations is bright when continuous improvement is at its core, ensuring that the journey toward equity remains dynamic, responsive, and ever-progressing. By placing continuous improvement at the center of their equity initiatives, organizations can move beyond compliance and toward a more just and inclusive future.

Case Study

Cultivating Equity: A Continuous Improvement Journey

A rapidly growing technology company is on a mission to embrace equity and inclusion as core values. They recognize that to remain competitive in a dynamic industry, they must foster an environment where diverse talent thrives. This case study explores this organization's ongoing journey toward equity, highlighting its continuous improvement efforts.

Background

Like many organizations, they struggled with diversity and inclusion. They had been focused on attracting top talent but had not paid equal attention to retaining and advancing that talent, leading to issues of representation and inclusion.

The Challenge

- **Lack of Diversity:** The organization had a predominantly male and homogenous workforce, especially in technical roles.

- **Inclusion Issues:** Employee surveys revealed that some minority groups felt excluded from key decision-making processes and company culture.

- **Retention and Advancement:** Women and underrepresented minorities were leaving the company at higher rates than their counterparts, leading to a loss of valuable talent.

The Continuous Improvement Journey

The organization recognized that achieving equity required more than a one-time effort. It required a continuous improvement mindset.

Phase 1: Data Collection (Year 1)

The organization began by collecting demographic data on its workforce, analyzing hiring practices, and reviewing promotion and compensation structures. They also initiated focus groups and surveys to understand employee experiences better.

Phase 2: Setting Goals (Year 2)

With a better understanding of their equity gaps, the organization set clear, measurable goals for improvement. These goals included increasing the percentage of underrepresented minorities in leadership roles, reducing gender pay gaps, and enhancing inclusion.

Phase 3: Implementation (Year 3)

The organization launched a series of initiatives aimed at addressing their challenges:

- **Revamped Hiring Practices:** Implemented blind resume screening and established diverse interview panels.

- **Inclusive Leadership Training:** Provided ongoing training for leaders to foster inclusive leadership behaviors.

- **Mentorship Programs:** Introduced mentorship programs to support the career development of underrepresented employees.

- **Diversity Recruitment Initiatives:** Actively participated in job fairs and outreach programs targeting minority candidates.

Phase 4: Continuous Feedback and Adaptation (Ongoing)

The organization created a continuous feedback loop by encouraging employees to voice concerns, suggestions, and experiences related to equity and inclusion. They established an equity committee responsible for reviewing progress and recommending adjustments to the strategies.

Results and Impact

After several years of continuous improvement efforts, the organization achieved significant milestones:

- **Diverse Workforce:** The percentage of underrepresented minorities in technical roles increased by 25%, and gender diversity improved notably in leadership positions.

- **Inclusion:** Employee surveys indicated improved feelings of inclusion and belonging, with many citing a more inclusive culture and greater transparency in decision-making.

- **Retention:** Employee retention improved across all demographics, reducing the turnover rate by 15%.

- **Market Reputation:** The organization's commitment to equity and continuous improvement was recognized in the industry, resulting in positive media coverage and an increase in the number of applications from diverse candidates.

The organization's continuous improvement journey in equity demonstrated that commitment to change, data-driven decision-making, and a willingness to adapt are vital elements in building a more inclusive and equitable organization. While their journey is ongoing, the results achieved so far show that embracing continuous improvement in equity is not just the right thing to do; it's a strategic imperative that benefits the company and its employees alike.

Integrative Exercise

Continuous Improvement for Equity

The objective of this integrative exercise is to help participants understand the concept of continuous improvement in the context of equity within organizations and to develop actionable strategies for fostering a culture of ongoing equity improvement.

Materials Needed

- Whiteboard or flip chart with markers.

- Sticky notes and pens/pencils for each participant.

- Handouts summarizing key points from "The Future of Equity in Organizations"

Step 1: Introduction (10 minutes)

- Begin by summarizing the key points from "The Future of Equity in Organizations"

- Explain that the objective of this exercise is to apply these principles to real-world scenarios.

Step 2: Scenario Exploration (15 minutes)

- Distribute handouts with a list of hypothetical scenarios related to equity issues within an organization. These scenarios could involve hiring practices, promotions, diversity training, or inclusion initiatives.

- Ask participants to read and discuss these scenarios in small groups (3-5 participants per group).

- In their groups, participants should identify areas within each scenario where continuous improvement for equity is needed and discuss potential strategies for improvement.

Step 3: Strategy Development (20 minutes)

- Reconvene as a larger group and ask each small group to share one scenario and the strategies they discussed for continuous improvement.

- As a collective group, create a list of actionable strategies for continuous improvement in equity. Write these on the whiteboard or flip chart.

Step 4: Reflection and Commitment (10 minutes)

- Have each participant individually reflect on one specific equity-related issue or challenge they have encountered or observed in their workplace.

- On sticky notes, participants should write down a strategy or action they commit to implementing to address this issue, inspired by the exercise discussion.

Step 5: Sharing and Accountability (10 minutes)

- Participants can choose to share their commitments with the larger group if they are comfortable.

- Emphasize the importance of accountability and encourage participants to follow through with their commitments.

Step 6: Closing Remarks (5 minutes)

- Summarize the key takeaways from the exercise, emphasizing the importance of continuous improvement in achieving equity goals within organizations.

- Thank participants for their engagement and commitment to fostering a more equitable workplace.

This integrative exercise encourages participants to actively engage with the concept of continuous improvement in equity and equips them with actionable strategies that can be applied in their workplaces. It promotes discussion, reflection, and a commitment to making meaningful change.

Chapter Fifteen

The Tripod Method

The Self Care Network LLC has pioneered a comprehensive approach to EIBD that goes beyond traditional methods. The Tripod Method is a robust framework designed to align the goals and initiatives of an organization at every level—from the board and executive leadership to the employees. This method is not only about advancing EIBD objectives but also about fostering a culture of self-care and mental wellness. By prioritizing communication, storytelling, and healing, we empower organizations to achieve sustainable growth and true inclusivity.

In the contemporary business environment, embracing the principles of EIBD is no longer optional—it is essential. Organizations that prioritize these values not only foster healthier work environments but also drive innovation, resilience, and sustainable success. At The Self Care Network LLC, we have developed a strategic approach that integrates EIBD into the very fabric of an organization. In this chapter, we will explore the core elements of our method, offering insights into how to begin this transformative journey. While we will not reveal every detail of our process here, we invite you to connect with us to learn more about how we can help your organization thrive.

The Importance of EIBD

Before diving into the specifics, it is crucial to understand why EIBD matters. Equity, inclusion, belonging, and diversity are not just abstract concepts; they are the pillars that support a strong, dynamic, and forward-thinking organization. These principles ensure that every individual, regardless of their background, has an equal opportunity to contribute, grow, and succeed. They foster an environment where diverse perspectives are valued, where everyone feels they belong, and where the organization as a whole can innovate and excel.

Implementing EIBD, however, is not without its challenges. It requires more than a few policy changes or a one-time training session. It demands a comprehensive, strategic approach that aligns EIBD with your organization's core values and long-term goals.

Core Principles of Our Approach

At the heart of our approach are four core principles: Equity, Inclusion, Belonging, and Diversity. Each of these principles plays a vital role in shaping an organization's culture and success. To review, let us take a closer look at each:

- **Equity** is about fairness and justice. It ensures that all individuals have access to the same opportunities, recognizing that some may need more support than others to achieve their full potential.

- **Inclusion** means creating a culture where all voices are heard and valued. It is about actively inviting diverse perspectives into the conversation and decision-making processes.

- **Belonging** is the sense that everyone is an integral part of the organization. When people feel they belong, they are more engaged, more committed, and more likely to contribute their best work.

- **Diversity** involves embracing and celebrating the wide range of differences that make each of us unique. This goes beyond just race or gender to include aspects like age, socioeconomic background, religion, disability, sexual orientation, and more.

These principles guide every aspect of our strategic approach. They are the foundation upon which we build a culture that not only supports but thrives on EIBD.

The Journey to EIBD: An Overview

While the journey to fully integrating EIBD into your organization is complex, it is also incredibly rewarding. Our strategic framework is designed to be comprehensive yet flexible, tailored to meet the unique needs of your organization. Here is a high-level overview of how The Self Care Network LLC works with organizations to fully integrate EIBD in organizations:

1. Establishing the Foundation

The first step in our approach is to embed EIBD principles into the very DNA of your organization. This involves developing a clear, organization-wide commitment to EIBD, starting with leadership, and extending it to every employee. It is about creating policies and practices that reflect your commitment to EIBD at every level.

2. Enhancing Representation and Leadership Diversity

Diversity is more than just a numbers game—it is about ensuring that leadership reflects the diversity of the communities you serve. At The Self Care Network LLC, we work with organizations to develop strategies that increase representation at all levels, particularly in leadership roles. This might involve creating diverse talent pipelines, revising hiring practices, and setting measurable targets to track progress.

3. Promoting Inclusive Leadership

Inclusive leadership is essential for creating a culture of belonging. We provide training and support to help leaders develop the skills they need to lead inclusively. This includes understanding how to recognize and mitigate bias, fostering a culture of open communication, and ensuring that diverse perspectives are included in decision-making.

4. Creating an Inclusive Work Environment

An inclusive environment is one where everyone feels welcome, respected, and valued. We help organizations identify barriers to inclusion and develop strategies to create a more inclusive workplace. This might involve revising policies, enhancing employee resource groups, or conducting regular climate surveys to assess the inclusivity of the work environment.

5. Fostering a Sense of Belonging

Belonging is the culmination of equity, inclusion, and diversity. It is the feeling that every individual is a valued member of the organization. We work with organizations to foster this sense of belonging through initiatives that promote community, celebrate diversity, and ensure that everyone feels connected to the organization's mission and goals.

6. Driving Equity Through Policies and Practices

Equity requires that we look closely at our policies and practices to identify and eliminate disparities. This might involve conducting an equity audit, revising compensation practices, or ensuring that professional development opportunities are distributed equitably. We help organizations make these critical changes, ensuring that equity is at the forefront of every decision.

7. Extending Impact Beyond the Organization

True commitment to EIBD extends beyond the walls of the organization. It is about making a positive impact on the broader community. We guide organizations in developing partnerships, advocating for social justice, and engaging with the community in ways that promote equity and inclusion on a larger scale.

Measuring Success: The Role of Key Performance Indicators

A critical part of our approach is ensuring that progress is measurable. We work with organizations to develop key performance indicators (KPIs) that track the success of EIBD initiatives. These might include metrics related to diversity representation, employee engagement, pay equity, or community impact. By regularly measuring and reporting on these KPIs, organizations can ensure that their EIBD efforts are not only effective but also sustainable.

The Tripod Method: A Holistic Approach to EIBD

The Tripod Method is the cornerstone of The Self Care Network LLC's approach to embedding EIBD into an organization's culture. It is a strategic, multi-faceted framework designed to ensure that every level of the organization—board, executive leadership, and employees—works in unison towards shared EIBD goals. The Tripod Method is not just about setting policies; it is about fostering a deep, sustainable change that permeates the entire organization, aligning everyone from the top down with the principles of equity and inclusion.

The Three Pillars of the Tripod Method

The Tripod Method is built on three interconnected pillars:
- Board Engagement and Leadership Commitment

- Executive Healing and Inclusive Leadership

- Employee Empowerment and Cultural Transformation

These three pillars are essential for creating a balanced and effective EIBD strategy. Like the legs of a tripod, each pillar supports the others, and all must be strong for the structure to stand.

Pillar 1: Board Engagement and Leadership Commitment

The first pillar of the Tripod Method focuses on engaging the board and securing leadership commitment to EIBD. For meaningful change to occur, it is crucial that those at the highest levels of the organization are not only on board but are also actively leading the charge.

Key Strategies

- **Initial Assessment**: We begin by conducting an initial EIBD Assessment with key stakeholders, including the board chair and executives. This helps us understand the organization's current EIBD efforts and identify areas for improvement.

- **Storytelling Circles**: We facilitate Storytelling Circles specifically tailored for board members and executives. These sessions allow leaders to share their personal and organizational narratives, deepening their understanding of EIBD and its impact on the organization. This also fosters emotional connections and a unified sense of purpose.

- **Ongoing Accountability**: EIBD goals and objectives are integrated into the board's strategic planning and leadership evaluations. This ensures that EIBD is not just a one-time initiative but a long-term commitment.

Pillar 2: Executive Healing and Inclusive Leadership

The second pillar focuses on the executive leadership team. Executives play a crucial role in shaping the organizational culture, and for EIBD initiatives to succeed, they must lead with authenticity, empathy, and inclusivity.

Key Strategies

- **Executive Healing Sessions**: Recognizing the unique pressures and responsibilities executives face, we provide healing sessions that address internalized biases, foster mental health, and promote resilience. These sessions are essential for helping leaders manage the emotional and psychological challenges of driving EIBD initiatives.

- **Inclusive Leadership Training**: We equip executives with the tools and knowledge needed to lead inclusively. This includes training on cultural competence, unconscious bias, and strategies for fostering an inclusive work environment. By focusing on self-care and personal growth, we prepare executives to lead EIBD efforts with a genuine commitment to equity and belonging.

Pillar 3: Employee Empowerment and Cultural Transformation

The third pillar is all about empowering employees and transforming the organizational culture. True inclusion and belonging can only be achieved when every employee feels valued, respected, and connected to the organization's mission.

Key Strategies

- **Cultural Competency Workshops**: We conduct immersive workshops and facilitated discussions designed to build cultural competence and self-awareness among employees. These sessions encourage personal reflection on bias, foster stronger workplace connections, and help employees align their personal and professional goals with the organization's EIBD objectives.

- **Employee Engagement and Feedback:** Regular climate surveys and feedback loops are established to gauge the inclusivity of the work environment and identify areas for improvement. Employee Resource Groups (ERGs) and other support networks are also encouraged to foster community and belonging within the organization.

How the Tripod Method Drives EIBD

The beauty of the Tripod Method lies in its holistic approach. By engaging the board, healing, and empowering executives, and transforming the employee experience, the method ensures that EIBD is woven into the fabric of the organization. Here is how the Tripod Method drives EIBD:

- **Unified Vision**: The Tripod Method ensures that the board, executives, and employees are aligned in their understanding and commitment to EIBD. This unified vision is critical for driving change and sustaining momentum.

- **Tailored Strategies**: The method is not one-size-fits-all. Each pillar is tailored to the specific needs and challenges of the organization, ensuring that the EIBD strategy is relevant and effective.

- **Sustainable Change**: By focusing on healing and empowerment, the Tripod Method addresses the root causes of exclusion and inequity, rather than just treating the symptoms. This leads to more sustainable, long-term change.

- **Continuous Improvement**: The method emphasizes ongoing assessment, feedback, and adjustment. This ensures that the organization continues to evolve and improve in its EIBD efforts, rather than stagnating after initial successes.

Conclusion: A Call to Action

The Tripod Method offers a comprehensive, integrated approach to EIBD that goes beyond surface-level initiatives. It is about creating deep, meaningful change that starts at the top and permeates every level of the organization. By engaging the board, healing, and empowering executives, and transforming the employee experience, the Tripod Method ensures that your organization not only meets its EIBD goals but thrives in an inclusive, equitable environment.

If you are ready to take your organization's commitment to EIBD to the next level, the Tripod Method provides the roadmap. We have shared the high-level concepts in this chapter, but the true power of the Tripod Method lies in its application. We invite you to connect with us to explore how the Tripod Method can be tailored to meet your organization's unique needs.

Are you ready to build a stronger, more inclusive organization? Let us take the next step together.

Visit us at www.theselfcarenetwork.org to learn more and to start your journey toward meaningful change.

Conclusion

In the journey through the pages of *Centering Equity in Your Organization*, we've embarked on a transformative exploration of what it means to embrace equity in the fabric of our workplaces. From understanding the foundational principles of diversity, equity, inclusion, and belonging to implementing actionable strategies that foster genuine inclusivity, this book serves as a compass guiding organizational leaders toward a future defined by equity and excellence.

As we reach the conclusion of this enlightening voyage, it's essential to reflect on the profound impact that centering equity can have on organizational culture, performance, and, ultimately, society at large. By prioritizing equity, we transcend mere compliance with regulations; we embrace a higher standard of ethical responsibility and social consciousness.

The insights shared within these pages are not merely theoretical constructs but actionable blueprints for transformation. They invite us to challenge conventional norms, to dismantle systemic barriers, and to champion the voices of those historically marginalized. They remind us that true progress stems from an unwavering commitment to justice and fairness.

As leaders, it is incumbent upon us to heed the call to action embedded within these words. We must recognize that the pursuit of equity is not a destination but an ongoing journey—one that requires courage, compassion, and collaboration. It demands that we interrogate our biases, confront our privileges, and champion the rights of every individual to thrive authentically within our organizations.

In closing, let us embrace the opportunity before us to be catalysts for change. Let us commit ourselves wholeheartedly to the noble cause of centering equity in our organizations, knowing that in doing so, we not only elevate our workplaces but also contribute to a more just and equitable world for generations to come.

Thank you for joining me on this transformative expedition. May the principles of equity guide your path, and may your organization be a beacon of inclusivity, empowerment, and hope for all.

With deepest gratitude,
Jenora Ledbetter
CEO/Founder
The Self Care Network LLC

About the Author

J enora Ledbetter, MA, serves as the Chief Executive Officer and founder of The Self Care Network LLC. Drawing upon her extensive expertise in advocacy and policy, Jenora possesses a nuanced understanding, particularly in Executive and Human Resources management, including discrimination laws and labor relations, cultivated over a span of more than a decade.

Equipped with a master's degree in advocacy and policy, complemented by a bachelor's degree in psychology, Jenora has fortified her capabilities as a certified Chief Diversity, Equity, and Inclusion Officer. Her professional journey is marked by a distinguished tenure as the former Regional Director of several non-profit organizations, where she orchestrated transformative strategies crucial in shaping the trajectory of these entities during pivotal phases of evolution.

Jenora Ledbetter's commitment to fostering inclusive environments and her adept leadership in navigating complex organizational landscapes underscore her instrumental role in driving forward the mission and vision of The Self Care Network LLC.

Certified across various disciplines, including diversity equity inclusion, and belonging, non-profit management, and employment and labor law, Jenora's multifaceted skill set underscores her commitment to fostering inclusive, equitable, and thriving organizational cultures. With an unwavering dedication to enhancing businesses and organizations, Jenora imparts her knowledge through courses on organizational behavior, leadership management, and cultural awareness and sensitivity.

Central to her ethos is the creation of environments fostering transformative growth, where individuals and organizations alike can achieve unparalleled performance. Jenora's leadership philosophy is grounded in the belief that diverse perspectives and inclusive practices are fundamental to organizational success. Her commitment to replacing restrictive protocols with frameworks that prioritize equity is a testament to her vision for progressive change.

Jenora authentically shares her personal journey, enriching her leadership approach with lived experiences. Through her advocacy and expertise, she catalyzes meaningful conversations and empowers others to embrace diversity and inclusion as core values. Jenora Ledbetter's leadership exemplifies a steadfast dedication to driving positive change and fostering environments where all individuals can thrive.

www.ingramcontent.com/pod-product-compliance
Lightning Source LLC
Chambersburg PA
CBHW062123020426
42335CB00013B/1077